Good Practice in Salon Management

Dawn Mernagh-Ward and Jennifer Cartwright

Stanley Thornes (Publishers) Ltd

First published in 1997 by:
Stanley Thornes (Publishers) Ltd
Ellenborough House
Wellington Street
CHELTENHAM
GL50 1YW
United Kingdom

97 98 99 00 01 / 10 9 8 7 6 5 4 3 2 1

A catalogue record for this book is available from the British Library.

ISBN 0–7487–2887–2

Cover photos: The Image Bank

Typeset by Florencetype Ltd, Stoodleigh, Devon
Printed and bound in Great Britain by Scotprint, Musselburgh

Foreword

Management skills are often daunting. Where do I start? Who should I ask? Where can I find the information I need? You need look no further than this book. It is clear, well written and packed full of useful ideas all of which work and can be used in practice.

If you are a qualified beauty therapist, complementary therapist or hairdresser; if you are a student taking NVQ Level III qualifications, or are embarking on a modern apprenticeship; or if you wish to start your own business or to improve the one you have – this is the book for you. It clearly explains:

- how to plan your salon – selecting the right salon, services, products, retailing and hygiene requirements
- how to staff your salon – choosing the right staff and keeping them through the use of various motivation techniques
- all the business laws you need to know – these are both up to date and sufficiently detailed
- how to market, advertise and make costings – in order to make yourself a profit!
- financial management – how to raise finance, analyse your business and keep the bank balance in the black.

Good Practice in Salon Management is packed with activities, questions to ask, points to note, plans and key terms.

When you buy this book it won't be resting on the bookshelf – it will be in everyday use. I cannot commend it highly enough.

Stephanie Henderson

Dedication

To our husbands, Ken and David, for their support, guidance, assistance and patience.

Contents

	Introduction	*vii*
	Acknowledgements	*viii*
Chapter 1	**Type and choice of business premises**	**1**
	Forms of business arrangements	1
	Choice and type of premises	5
	Basic business legislation	8
Chapter 2	**Physical resource planning**	**10**
	Salon layout	10
	Services to be offered	13
	Products and equipment	14
	Retailing and stock control	16
	Hygiene in the salon/clinic environment	24
Chapter 3	**Human resources (staff selection, recruitment and appraisal)**	**31**
	Establishing the needs of the business	31
	Organisational structure	32
	Roles, responsibilities and qualities of staff	33
	Recruitment	48
	Contract of employment	61
	Induction	63
	Appraisal	67
	Staff development	70
Chapter 4	**Business legislation**	**72**
	Employment legislation	72
	Treatment and consumer legislation	87
Chapter 5	**Marketing and promotion**	**92**
	Corporate image	92
	Marketing	94
	Costing of services	95
	Advertising, promotion and publicity	97
	Marketing strategies	101

Chapter 6   **Management theories and style**   **110**

The importance of theories   110
Organisational theory   110
Motivation theories   111
Leadership theories   120
Communication mechanisms   121
Team roles   123
Practical and effective management techniques   124

Chapter 7   **Business terminology and financial management**   **138**

Insurance   138
Taxation   141
Raising finance   143
Basic business terminology   144
Book-keeping and computerised account systems   146

Chapter 8   **Management of the business**   **155**

Analysing your position   155
Type of business   156
Buying an existing business   156
Formulating the business plan   157
Budgeting/achieving profit   158
Salary structures   164
Business analysis – the strategic plan   164
Pitfalls of business   165
Reviewing, evaluating and moving forward   167
Case studies   167

Glossary of terms   **172**

Index   **176**

Introduction

Hairdressing, beauty and holistic therapies offer extremely diverse career opportunities, particularly in today's expanding service industry markets.

Most people entering these exciting fields aim at some time to become self-employed, whether through owning a business and employing others, or working on their own. This is achievable providing they are skilled, enthusiastic, determined, eager to learn and research their market thoroughly. In order to maximise business potential all areas and aspects of business should be considered thoroughly prior to setting up and should be continually monitored, reviewed and evaluated. It is extremely important to remember that legislation will vary from time to time and it is the owner's responsibility to check that the business is operating according to current legislation.

Good Practice in Salon Management is intended as a guide for hairdressers, beauty therapists and holistic practitioners intending to set up in business and for those who are already self-employed.

Wishing you success and happiness in your business.

Dawn Mernagh-Ward

Jennifer Cartwright

Acknowledgements

We wish to express our thanks to our husbands, our families and friends for their support and encouragement whilst researching and writing this book.

Special thanks to: Paul Atherton and Graham Fabes (Carlton Professional), BABTAC, Delvis Bona, British Acupuncture Council, Elizabeth Cartwright (East Midlands College), John Claughton (Wella), James Crebbin-Bailey and staff at Total Look in Epsom, Melissa Daniels and Sharon Williamson (International Dermal Institute), Jaynie Fisher, Moira Paulusz and Sasha Lill (Health and Beauty Salon), Oriele Frank (Elemis UK Ltd), Sheila Godfrey, Laurence Green (E.A. Ellisons), John Harrington (Phytomer), Stephanie Henderson, Kate Jenkins (Inverness UK Ltd), Dean Lander, Leicestershire Guild of the Disabled, Gary Puxty (Hairdressing and Beauty Equipment Centre), Stephen McDonald (Solihull College), Judy Naake and Norman Oley (Caplin Naake Associates), National Hairdressers' Federation, Elisabeth Peet, Vicky Schaveien (Steiner Training Ltd), Aarti Shah, Mike Shirley (Sothys), Pamela Stevens, Tisserand Aromatherapy, Toni & Guy, Stewart Ward and staff at Blushers in Coventry, Gaye Wensley and Brian Wildman (Bellitas).

We are extremely grateful to our colleagues in the complementary therapies, hairdressing and beauty industries, in particular to the companies and associations that have kindly allowed us to reproduce logos, photographs and illustrations.

Figure 5.1	BABTAC
Figure 5.3	Blushers Hair & Beauty Salon, Coventry
Figure 5.3	Bonaroma Hair & Beauty Salon, Rotherham
Figures 5.1 and 5.4	British Acupuncture Council
Figures 2.13 and 5.5	Caplin Naake Associates
Figure 5.3	Dean Lander
Figures 7.5 & 8.4	E.A. Ellisons Ltd
Figure 5.3	Electrolysis Health & Beauty Clinic, Knowle
Figure 3.6	Elemis UK Ltd
Figure 3.16	Sheila Godfrey
Figure 2.11	Hairdressing and Beauty Equipment Centre
Figures 3.12, 5.1 and 5.6	Health & Beauty Salon
Figures 7.1, 7.2, 7.6 and 8.3	Inverness UK Ltd
Figures 5.1 and 5.4	National Hairdressers' Federation
Figure 8.7	Pamela Stevens
Figure 4.1	Pat Shirreff-Thomas, Ovation Productions, London
Figure 5.3	Aarti Shah
Figure 5.1	Sothys
Figures 3.2 and 4.1	Steiners Training Ltd.

Figure 8.4   Stephen McDonald, Solihull College
Figures 1.2, 2.2 and 5.1   Tony & Guy
Figure 2.4   Tisserand Aromatherapy
Figure 2.1   Virgin Atlantic
Figures 5.1, 8.5 and 8.6   Wella

1 Type and choice of business premises

This chapter covers the following areas:
- ➤ forms of business arrangements
- ➤ choice and type of premises
- ➤ basic business legislation.

Hairdressing, beauty and holistic therapies are diverse and exciting careers offering many opportunities and working arrangements. There are few professions where so much choice is available. It is essential that the practitioner, whether a junior manager or self-employed, has a good working knowledge of salon administration and related legislation as the success of the salon ultimately depends on efficient working practices. Different countries have differing legislation governing business practices.

Forms of business arrangements

Legally all businesses fall into one of the following categories:
- sole trader
- partnership
- limited company (private and public)
- franchise
- co-operative.

Sole trader

A sole trader is the simplest form of business organisation. One person controls the finance and all of the decisions. From a legal point of view there is nothing that needs to be done to set up in business as a sole trader. This is one of the most popular forms of business arrangement for the practitioner in the health, beauty and hairdressing industries. As a sole trader you are classed by the Inland Revenue as self employed.

Advantages
- Easy to set up – no lengthy legal formalities.
- Total control of the business.
- Immediate decision making.
- Taxed as an individual/self assessment.
- Should benefit from close relations with suppliers.
- Easy to wind up.

1

Fig. 1.1 *Home visiting therapist*

Disadvantages

- Liable for any business losses.
- No legal distinction between the business and personal assets.
- Possible lack of continuity in management if the owner is ill.
- Does not have status.
- Possible lack of finances for expansion.

Partnership

By definition a partnership is when two or more people go into business together without registering as a limited company or a co-operative.

Again this form of business can be set up without legal formalities, but this is not to be recommended as severe disagreements could jeopardise the business. It is much safer to have a formal partnership agreement drawn up detailing the roles and responsibilities of all partners.

Advantages

- A good way to start up a business that requires more capital than one person alone may have.
- Wider range of complementary skills and knowledge.
- Sharing of workload and general pressures of running a business.
- Sharing of any business losses.

Disadvantages

- All partners are responsible for any business debts even if they are caused by the actions of the others.
- Legal costs are involved in drawing up a partnership agreement.

- Death or bankruptcy of one partner will automatically dissolve the partnership (unless previous arrangements have been made).
- Possible personality clashes can cause problems.

Private limited company

A private limited company is formed with a minimum of two share-holders, one of whom must be a director. A company secretary must also be appointed but he/she can be an outsider.

This is a company whereby any business debts are limited to the amount put in to the business. Therefore if the business does go bankrupt, personal possessions cannot be taken to pay the company's debts.

Prior to registration a limited company must produce and adhere to the following two legal documents:

- Memorandum of Association – this sets out the objectives of the company, as well as the company's share capital.
- Articles of Association – this sets out additional rules by which the company will be governed.

Public limited company

A public limited company has to have at least seven shareholders with no maximum limit. The shares are sold on the stock exchange and the company has to abide by the rules and regulations of the 'Authority of Exchange' and the legal requirements laid down by the Department of Trade and Industry.

Shareholders

A shareholder is the name given to a person who quite simply has a share in the company. Each shareholder puts a given amount of capital into the company and in return receives a share of the profits that the company makes. Shareholders elect a 'Board of Directors' to act on their behalf or, in the case of small companies, use important shareholders on the board itself. Such shareholders can be employed by the business, in which case they are referred to as working directors as opposed to executive directors.

Types of shares

There are two types of shares:

1 Ordinary or equity shares
   These are high risk shares as any company losses are divided equally between the holders of such shares. However, any revenues from profit, or 'dividends' as they are known, are also shared in this manner.

2 Preference shares
   This type of share gives the holder a preferential right to a reasonable level of dividend set at a percentage of the profits. Only when the preference shareholders have received their percentage will ordinary shareholders receive theirs.

Advantages

- Limited liability.
- Capital may be increased selling shares.
- Better definition of management structures.
- Business not affected by death or bankruptcy of any of its share-holders.
- Higher level of status.
- Shareholders are employees of the company and therefore entitled to DSS benefits should the need arise.

Disadvantages

- Costly to set up with time-consuming legal formalities.
- The business will have to make public its accounts.
- As an employee of the company you will be subject to PAYE (see Chapter 7).

Franchise

A franchise is a business relationship between a franchiser (the owner of a name or method of business) and a franchisee (an operator of that business). The franchisee agrees to pay the franchiser a sum of money for the use of the business name, method of doing business etc. Often there is an initial fee and an agreed percentage of sales afterwards.

Fig. 1.2 A *franchise salon*

Advantages

- A tried and tested formula.
- A corporate image is instantly recognisable.
- Normally there is a wealth of knowledge available concerning most aspects of the business.
- Back up services normally provided.
- Sharing of advertising costs.

Disadvantages

- Normally very expensive to set up.
- The business is never truly your own.
- The franchiser may lay down certain requirements.
- May not be a flexible enough system to cater for changing needs of a local market.
- Profits normally have to be shared with the franchiser.

Co-operative

A co-operative is a business that is owned and controlled by the people working in it, therefore membership is usually open to all employees. The profits are not shared on the basis of the amount of capital put into the business by each individual but are distributed in proportion to the amount of work done by each person.

ACTIVITY	Try to find examples of each of the different types of business category in your neighbourhood.

Choice and type of premises

When setting up in business one of the first things you will need to think about is the premises. The type and location of the premises are extremely important and it will be essential to research this thoroughly. First, you will need to establish that there is going to be a suitable potential market where you are looking. Local competitors will also need to be taken into account, as will parking facilities and neighbouring businesses – you hardly want a relaxing health clinic situated next door to a betting office or fish and chip shop! Also, will the site attract passing trade and is it in a safe enough area for women to feel comfortable coming for treatments in the evening? If the premises you are interested in are not already occupied as a salon you will need to apply to the local council for a change of use.

POINT TO NOTE ▷ *Never agree to take on premises until you have ensured that is possible to change the use.*

You then need to decide whether you are going to buy or rent premises. Probably finances will dictate your ultimate choice, but remember that sometimes large shopping complexes are owned by large companies or councils and this may affect your choice.

Property advisors

When deciding on the choice and type of premises that you will require for your business you will need to obtain the expert advice of estate agents, surveyors and solicitors. Most commercial estate agents will be able to give invaluable information about the type of property available in their area. Solicitors will need to become involved once a deal is underway. Their role is to perform land searches and draw up contracts in the case of purchasing, or to go through all the clauses in the case of a leasehold agreement. Surveyors will need to carry out a structural survey on the intended premises and this is a good idea whether you are purchasing or leasing as many leasehold clauses include maintenance of the property and this can include parts of its structure. All property advisors should have one thing in common and that is to be able to help you negotiate the best possible terms. This normally means a favourable reduction in the cost of the purchase price or leasehold rent and terms. Remember that market conditions go in 'swings and roundabouts' and you as the purchaser may have the upper hand, so try not to appear too eager even if you have just found the perfect location as this will diminish your bargaining power.

Buying

If you decide that you are going to buy your premises you will need to contact a solicitor immediately to deal with the contracts involved and also to organise a land search. This is to check the ownership of the property and any plans in the future for redevelopment etc. You will also need to establish if the property is freehold, which means that the land and building would be yours if you purchased it, or whether it is leasehold, which means that the building would be yours but the land that it is built on belongs to a third party and you would need to pay a ground rent.

Renting

Renting, or leasing as it is correctly known, is when you agree to occupy a building in return for an agreed sum of money. If you decide to rent a property you will again need the services of a solicitor to draw up lease agreement which should include the following:

- how much rent is to be paid and how often (monthly, quarterly etc.)
- when the amount of rent paid will be reviewed
- how long the lease will run for
- who will be responsible for repairs, upkeep and decoration of the premises both internally and externally
- what are the rules regarding subletting
- awareness of the Landlord and Tenant Act (1954) (see later in this chapter)

Sub-leasing

Sub-leasing is when an existing tenant leases his property or part of it to a third party, e.g. a hairdresser leasing part of the property to a beauty therapist. It is not always possible to do this as there are usually strong restrictions on sub-letting in the contract. It would always be advisable to make sure the landlord is prepared to give permission to sub-leasing.

Altering premises

Whether you are the owner of the property or just leasing if you wish to alter the premises you will need to check the following:

- planning permission
- building and fire regulations
- Offices, Shops and Railway Premises Act (1963) (see later in this chapter).

POINT TO NOTE ▷ *Before setting up in business it is essential to prepare a business plan, particularly if financial support is needed. Most banks and financial institutions offer guidance and support for small businesses. A business plan should include:*

- *personal details*
- *type of business*
- *background of the business, e.g. staff, outgoings etc.*
- *products/services*
- *business market*
- *financial considerations/projections*
- *anticipated profits over a number of years (see Chapter 8).*

Choice of business name

One of the most important aspects in setting up in business is what to call it. A business name will be one of the first impressions given out and can have a direct effect on the success of the business. Whatever name is chosen it will need to be registered with the Companies Registration Office. First, it will be necessary to make sure that the name in mind is not already being used by an existing business or that it does not give the impression of being linked to a well known name. The Companies Registration Office produces a booklet giving guidance notes on business names. Any partners trading under a business name must show their own name and the address of the business on all stationery to be used by the business.

POINT TO NOTE ▷ *It is not normally necessary for a sole trader to register a business name but some may choose to do so. This is because if the business becomes successful another person could take the name and register it for themselves leaving the original person liable to change their business name.*

ACTIVITY

Try to think of an appropriate name for:

(a) a high-class hairdressing salon

(b) a beauty salon in a small rural village

(c) an aromatherapy clinic

(d) a multi-faceted complementary clinic in a smart town.

Basic business legislation

The Landlord and Tenant Act (1954)

This piece of legislation gives the tenant security of tenure which means that you cannot be removed from the premises you are leasing unless the landlord can show a justified reason (e.g. not paying the rent). If the landlord wishes to remove you to sell the premises you will be entitled to compensation.

Offices, Shops and Railway Premises Act (1963)

This piece of legislation relates in particular to hygiene, health and safety of the premises and covers such things as:

- washing facilities
- toilets for both sexes and for client use
- sanitation
- safety on stairways
- eating and drinking facilities for staff required to stay on the premises at break-times
- adequate space for each employee
- fire exits and adequate fire fighting equipment.

Electricity at Work Regulations Act (1990)

This piece of legislation states that all pieces of electrical equipment in the workplace should be checked annually by a qualified electrician. In particular you should discontinue using any equipment that is broken or damaged, displays exposed wires or worn flexes or has a cracked or broken plug and you should never overload sockets.

This act only applies to businesses that employ people who work over 21 hours per week.

Law of Property Act (1995)

This Act supersedes the previous law of 1925 and is applicable to new leases only. This reduces anxiety to the leaseholder if it is decided with the landlord's approval to reassign the lease. The previous law enabled the landlord to go back to the original leaseholder if the assignee defaulted on rental payments.

Disability Discrimination Act (1995)

This Act has several clauses and one of these makes it unlawful for people letting or selling land or property to discriminate against disabled people. Most premises, including land, houses, flats and business premises are covered by the Act. This does not mean that the person selling has to alter the premises to make them more accessible, but only that the person interested in buying should not be discriminated against because of a disability. However, a business occupying leasehold property may ask the landlord for permission to make the premises more accessible. This must be granted unless there is good reason not to.

KEY TERMS

You need to know what these words and phrases mean. Go back through the chapter to find out.

Sole trader
Partnership
Limited company (private and public)
Franchise
Co-operative
Property advisors

Buying
Renting
Sub-leasing
Altering premises
Business name
Basic business legislation

2 Physical resource planning

This chapter covers the following areas:
➤ salon layout for the beauty and holistic therapist
➤ salon layout for the hairdresser
➤ services to be offered
➤ products and equipment
➤ retailing and stock control
➤ hygiene in the salon/clinic environment.

Physical resource planning is the sophisticated term given to the planning of the salon layout and the type of services to be offered. It also includes product and equipment choice. All of these areas are of tremendous importance to the overall success of a business and are worth some considerable thought. Visit as many existing businesses as possible, perhaps as a 'client', to get an overall feel for what works and what does not.

Be sure to look at all options as expensive mistakes can be hard to rectify later on, particularly in the case of salon layout.

Salon layout

Salon layout for the beauty and holistic therapist

The layout of the salon will to some extent have to tie in with the layout of the premises but it is essential to think long and hard about how you wish to conduct your business. Important points to consider are privacy for all treatment areas together with as little noise as possible. Prominent and eye-catching reception and display areas are important. First impressions really do count so it is paramount that the reception area is inviting to the client. The seating should be comfortable in order to allow the client to begin relaxing before the treatment commences. Staff and stock areas should be as unobtrusive as possible and securely locked if valuables are to be stored there. Laundry facilities will have to be considered if carried out in-house and again noise from washing machines must not interfere with the clinic atmosphere.

Heating, ventilation and lighting must be carefully organised, as the clinic will need to be at a comfortable temperature at all times and, especially where body treatments are being carried out, the client cannot be allowed to feel at all cold. Lighting should create a relaxing environment with the use of dimmer switches being highly recommended as strong bright lights can be very distracting to clients. There should be a sufficient air flow through the clinic to prevent the build up of airborne bacteria and odours such as those from the chemicals used in nail extensions, or a build up of essential oils for example. The airflow should also ensure that stagnant air, saturated with carbon dioxide due to exhalation from clients and therapists, is removed. Poor air quality is known to cause illness and lethargy. Client and staff washrooms/toilet facilities should ideally be separate from each other and should also accommodate both males and females. A knowledge of the Offices, Shops and Railway Premises Act is essential in the planning of the clinic layout (see Chapter 1).

When planning the colour scheme of the clinic the practitioner should spend a great deal of time considering the decor (wall and floor coverings, towels etc.) to ensure that the right sort of environment is created. Most beauty practitioners select warms colours, e.g. peaches, or relaxing colours such as greens. The type of client will play a large role in the selection of the colour scheme, e.g. it would be inappropriate to have a mixed gender clinic decorated in what are considered feminine colours such as pinks. Colour used in a superficial form such as in decor, towels and lighting can contribute to the client's relaxation and enjoyment of the clinic and should therefore be considered when planning the overall effect.

Fig. 2.1 *Hair and beauty salon*

Salon layout for the hairdresser

The hairdressing salon will have different requirements from the beauty or holistic clinic in the sense that it will need to be much more open in layout. It should have a prominent and eye-catching reception and display area with comfortable seating. The main body of the salon will then be designated as styling areas with provision for a consultation

11

before any treatment commences. The styling areas may consist of chairs facing mirrors hung on the walls or 'island' units which are normally double backed and make extra use of the 'middle space' in a salon. The siting of electric sockets will need to be carefully thought out as each area will need at least two power points, one for the hairdrier and one for curling /straightening tongs which need to be ready to use where necessary. The salon will need to have some form of shampoo area and this again may be in the form of an island unit where the shampooist can stand behind the sink or, if space is a problem, then sinks may need to be butted against a wall with the person working from the side. It is possible to purchase portable washing basins that can be moved into the treatment area for shampooing. This can be extremely useful where space is a problem and there would be no room for a shampooing area. In all cases it will be important to consider 'time and motion' (see p. 13).

It will be necessary to have a dispensary area where tints etc. are stored under COSHH regulations and mixed (see Chapter 4). This area will need to be away from direct sunlight and to be kept fairly cool. It may also be a place where stock is kept. The staff will need a private area and this if possible should be well away from all treatment areas as there may be personal belongings stored there. Laundry and washroom facilities need careful planning and as with all other types of salon/clinic, toilets should be separate for clients and staff. Heat developing equipment areas will have to be carefully thought out. It may be that the salon chooses to use portable equipment that can be wheeled into each treatment area or it may be necessary to designate certain fixed areas for such equipment. Heating, ventilation and lighting will call for careful consideration.

Fig. 2.2   *Hairdressing salon*

The salon will need to feel comfortable in temperature without being too hot, as there is the added heat from hairdriers. The salon will need excellent lighting ideally having spotlights over each area and possibly mirror lighting. It will also need efficient ventilation to prevent a build-up of strong odours from perm solutions and to prevent condensation forming on the windows.

POINT TO NOTE ▷ *In the Far East shampooing is considered a relaxing part of the service offered and is given whilst the client is lying down, with the emphasis being on comfort.*

GOOD PRACTICE ▷ *When planning the positioning of retail stock it is sadly essential in this day and age to think about shoplifting. Whilst you want the products to be eye-catching and accessible it is important that they are not too accessible. Short of storing them behind locked glass doors, which can be intimidating and time-consuming to open, it may be necessary to use only dummies or sample products for display unless you can afford a sophisticated 'tagging' system.*

Time and motion

This is the term given to the study of the length of time it takes to move from one work area to another. This can make a big difference to the efficiency of any business. For example, if the practitioner has to walk a long way from the reception area to the treatment area to the washbasin and back to the treatment area, and then fetch equipment stored elsewhere, this will waste time and create inefficiency. When setting up the salon layout it is worth giving some thought to time and motion studies as ultimately this could save money.

ACTIVITY

Decide on a particular type of salon and design the layout taking into consideration both 'time and motion' planning and other important features such as reception , stock rooms etc. Gather together swatches of fabrics and wall coverings that would be appropriate for the image to be created.

Services to be offered

One of the most important things to be considered when setting up the practice is the range of services to be offered. It may be that you are qualified in all aspects of the type of treatments that you are intending to offer or you may be thinking of employing 'specialists' such as an aromatherapist or a nail technician. Many clinics today are multifaceted and it is not uncommon to find hairdressers, beauty therapists and holistic practitioners working alongside each other. After all many of the clients will be having a whole range of these treatments in any case so it will broaden the client base for all concerned. Whatever you intend to offer in the way of services it is essential that market research is carried out (see Chapter 5) to ensure that the area in which you will operate is appropriate to the range of treatments available. Understanding your clients is one of the most important points in the ultimate success of a business.

Products and equipment

Once you have established the type and range of treatments that you intend to offer you next need to consider product and equipment choice. For both areas the market is enormous as you can see by glancing through a trade journal.

Most practitioners through the course of their careers will have worked with various product ranges and therefore have a preference as to what they would like to work with.

Product choice in beauty therapy

It is worth offering more than one range of skin care etc. if finances allow as in this way you are able to cater to different financial budgets. You will need to look at the diversity of the products in a skin care range, e.g. do they offer face, body, bust and hand and nail products or will you have to go elsewhere for some of these? Are the products only supplied through networked salons or can a client get replacements from the local department store? Does the company offer good back-up and can you order in small amounts or are there minimum order levels? What are the profit margins like? Some products have as much as a 50% mark up while others have much smaller percentages.

Does the company offer regular training courses and are these held in your area or will you have to travel a long way with added time and expense? Will the company be selective in who they supply their products to or can just about anyone sell them? Does the company offer group advertising or help individual salons with promotion events by supplying a representative from the company? Are the products sold via represen-tatives or stocked at the local hair and beauty wholesalers? Does the company offer free samples which will help to boost sales or do you have to pay for them ? What are their terms and conditions with regard to payment, bulk orders, return of faulty products etc.? Are the products going to appeal to a wide range of clients and to both men and women?

One of the best ways of deciding which range or ranges to take on board is to attend the many trade shows organised both nationally and interna-tionally. Most of the skin care companies exhibit at such events and many provide demonstrations and offer product testing.

Equipment choice guidelines

The choice of equipment available can make selection a difficult problem and again you will need to ask yourself lots of questions. There is a variety of equipment manufactured internationally to meet the demands of this fast expanding industry. The majority of companies produce a full range of electrical equipment, although some do specialise in one area.

Each supplier offers equipment at differing prices according to the development design on offer and the back-up services available. When selecting equipment the practitioner should carefully consider the treatments that can best be offered within the salon along with the available budget. Once this is decided it is wise to attend exhibitions, read trade journals and to liaise through professional associations with other practitioners before deciding which manufacturer's items to purchase. If possible, try to visit equipment showrooms to compare choice, range and availability of equipment. The following are the key questions that should be considered before any decisions are made.

- Is the practitioner to offer salon-based or home visiting services?
- Where is the equipment to be used and stored
- How much space is available for equipment presentation and storage?
- Would mobile or fixed wall-mounted equipment suit the environment better?
- Would a multi-purpose unit be more beneficial if there is a shortage of storage space ? (This could also be used as a point of sale for other treatments. However, if it is the only piece of equipment what will happen if it breaks down or needs to be serviced?)
- If the equipment needs to be carried in and out of cupboards, is it lightweight?
- Are any electrodes stored with the machine in a purpose designed area or separately? How will this suit the salon environment?
- What is the durability of the equipment? How often will it need servicing and where will this take place – on or off site? How long will it take? What will it cost?
- What training is offered by the company? Is this included in the price? Where will it take place?
- What back-up services are offered by the company? Do they provide training manuals or telephone support? Do they charge for these services?
- What is the reputation of the company? Are they long established? Do they attend the major international exhibitions? Are they active in more than one country?
- If purchasing from overseas, is the equipment compatible for use in the UK? (e.g. check the wiring and voltage, repair and replacement of accessories etc.)
- Have items of equipment have been manufactured in accordance with current European directives (EU countries only)?

Only once you have ensured positive responses to the above ideas should you proceed to buy all the necessary equipment. It is also possible to lease some of the more expensive pieces and this may be an option worth considering.

ACTIVITY

Gather together information on product and equipment ranges from well-known suppliers. Compare the services offered, prices and general back-up given.

Fig. 2.3 Hair and beauty wholesaler

Product choice in hairdressing

In the hairdressing salon it is normal to use only one or two ranges of products and this will probably be influenced by personal choice. It is important to make sure that the company offers good back-up facilities and that ordering is straightforward and efficient. The retail range may be different from the treatment range and will often come with some form of display shelving.

ACTIVITY	Gather together information on hairdressing products to compare prices, product range and company back-up.

Product choice in holistic therapies

In the holistic therapy clinic it may be the case that only minimal products and equipment are needed but if not then the above guidelines will apply.

Retailing and stock control

Retailing products and services

Selling is essential if a business is to survive. Profits made on the sales of products and services make the business successful which will ultimately increase the earning potential of all the employees.

It is therefore important for all employees to have a thorough understanding of all the products and treatments available within the business.

16

POINT TO NOTE ▷

The majority of cosmetic companies offer product knowledge workshops to familiarise the staff with their products and methods. If these are not available then it will be essential to ensure that all employees read all the information available about the products the business intends to sell.

GOOD PRACTICE ▷

Here are ten guidelines for successful selling.

1 *Find out exactly what the client needs. This means asking questions and listening carefully to the answers.*

   Use 'closed' questions to get short, straightforward answers (usually yes or no). These help to confirm or eliminate information and ideas.

   Use 'open' questions to invite fuller and more detailed answers. Open questions help to develop the conversation and provide more personal information.

2 *Give the client advice. Always relate the benefits of the product specifically to the client.*

3 *Always smile and talk confidently and positively about the product chosen. Where possible tell the client about your personal experiences with the product.*

4 *Explain how the product should be used. If possible let the client feel, smell or hold the product. Remember that if the client touches the product and asks the price, then the item is practically sold.*

5 *Close the sale. Look for signals that tell you the client has decided to take your advice and buy the product: head nodding in agreement, smiles and friendly eye contact are positive buying signals.*

6 *Where appropriate, explain the benefits of the different sizes available in the product. These will usually be linked to the price. Hesitation or reluctance to mention the price will give the client the impression that you consider the product too expensive.*

7 *Gain agreement with the client. This is achieved either immediately or after a short period of 'thinking' time. Do not be afraid of silences at this stage. Just keep quiet and wait patiently for the client to make a decision. Do not talk yourself out of a sale.*

8 *Use link selling to encourage your client to buy complementary products from the same range, e.g. cleansers and toners, body exfoliants and lotions etc.*

9 *Once you have sold the product, wrap it up and process the payment. As you hand over the purchase, check once more that the client understands how to use the product.*

10 *Enter the details of the purchase on the client's record card and be sure to ask next time how the client is finding the product.*

Sales and selling pointers

● Offer samples where possible – most people like to try a product before they buy it and if it is good they will be back to buy.

17

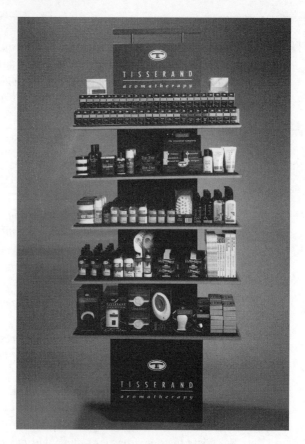

Fig. 2.4 *Retail display area*

- Introduce a friend to the salon scheme – if a regular client introduces a friend both should be given some incentive such as a slight discount or a gift etc.
- Acknowledge all client's birthdays – in the month of their birthday send each client an incentive to visit the salon/clinic.
- Organise new treatment promotions.
- Have new treatment information printed and hand this out to every client.
- Offer special treatment packages for holidays, Christmas etc.
- Change display areas very regularly.
- Change salon/clinic pricelists yearly and date them.
- Change salon/clinic decor regularly.
- Set out to promote a product every week knowing all its benefits, effects and ingredients (you will soon know your whole range very thoroughly).
- Organise a salon anniversary promotion yearly inviting local press along.
- Make a feature out of a 'slow' day of the week. Give it a name and offer extra incentives when people have an appointment on that day.
- Change your own image regularly.

Maintaining stock and the retail area

In many businesses stock taking and ordering are undertaken by the receptionist, but it may be a task given to a practitioner or manager. It is extremely important that retail products are accessible and that a good stock level is maintained to prevent loss of sales and of an important source of income.

Whoever is responsible for the business stock must:

- Keep the retail area clean and tidy: the counter, shelves and stock should be dusted every day and where possible have regular changes of display. Stock which is grubby and dusty will lose its value.

- Inform clients of current promotion: the attention of the clients should be drawn to special offers and the promotional material should be displayed where it will catch the client's eye.

- Carry out stock checks: stock checks should be carried out weekly to monitor how well different products are selling and to make sure that popular lines are re-ordered before being sold out.

- Price the retail products: identical products must not be priced differently. Price tickets should be checked as part of the regular stock checks. Old price tickets should be removed before putting on new ones so that a lower price is not disguised.

- Store stock correctly so that that it does not deteriorate or become damaged. Keep fast moving lines at the front of the shelves and slower moving ones nearer the back. Do not block aisles or passageways with containers of stock; keep it in a locked cupboard or secure room.

- Display stock attractively: displays should be set up with the minimum disruption to business. If all retail stock is to be displayed, extra space is needed for the fastest selling lines. Shelving should be clean, safe and undamaged and strong enough to take the weight of the products on display. Packaging should be displayed with the product. Take care with flimsy packaging and stack heavier goods lower down than more fragile items.

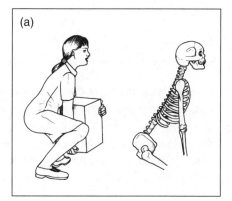 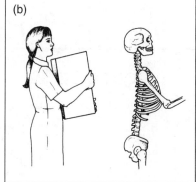

Fig. 2.5 *Correct lifting (a) and carrying (b) technique; avoid straining your back when moving heavy stock*

POINTS TO NOTE ▷

- Use 'dummy' stock under bright lighting: this way the colour, texture and fragrance of the products will not become spoiled.
- Be careful when unpacking stock. Look out for sharp staple fastenings on boxes and avoid using a knife. Protect your overall when carrying large items and mind those nails! Paper and cardboard packages should be flattened before disposal.

GOOD PRACTICE ▷

- Storing stock in straight lines makes counting easier.
- Keep accurate stock records. The quality of a product cannot be guaranteed once its expiry date has passed. Stock which has been stored beyond its 'shelf-life' has either to be sold off cheaply or ideally disposed of.
- Store stock in a cool dark place.
- Do not pile boxes too high.
- When an order arrives, bring old stock to the front and store new stock behind. This method of stock control is called FIFO, i.e. first in, first out.

POINTS TO NOTE ▷

- The business loses money on old stock which is sold off cheaply or thrown away. Products which are approaching their expiry date should be identified at the stock check and steps taken to sell them before its too late. This may mean offering a special promotion or reducing the price slightly as an incentive to buy.
- Take care when dismantling a display. Put back equipment where it will not become damaged and keep tools and accessories safe in a box.

GOOD PRACTICE ▷

- Ensure a good system of stock control is implemented highlighting the item, size, minimum and maximum levels of stock required.
- Review the stock control system regularly as requirements may fluctuate due to things such as: the time of year, promotions and changes in current trends. Seek advice from product suppliers who will have experience of these matters. They may also be helpful in providing a useful stock control system.
- Ensure stock is available or sales will be lost!

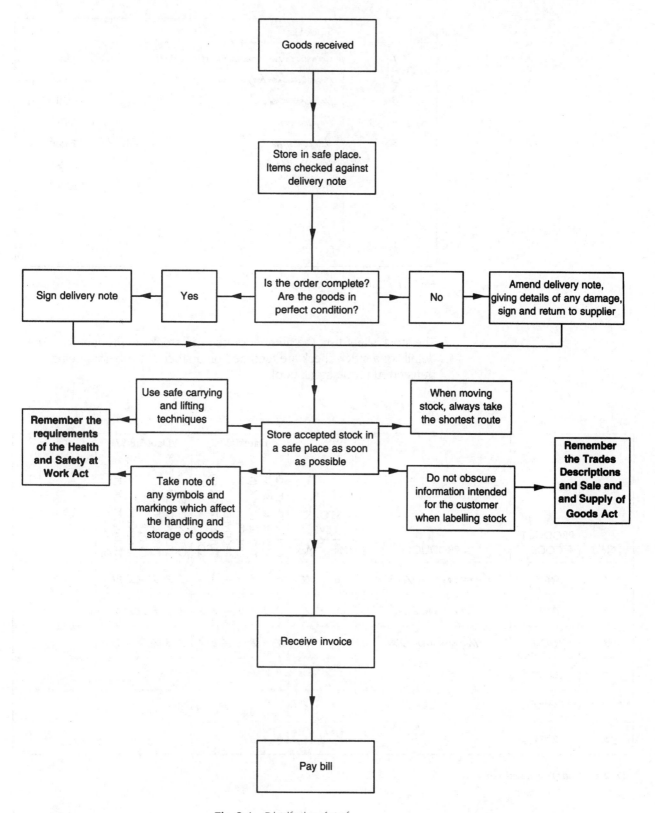

Fig. 2.6 *Distribution of stock*

	Stock List	
1	Aromatic oil for vapouriser or steam cabinet	30ml
2	Aromatic oil for body massage	30ml
3	Desincrustation gel	250g
4	Dry shampoo	250ml
5	Dry conditioner	250ml
6	Pre-perm shampoo	500ml
7	Anti-oxin conditioner	500ml
8		
9		
10		

Fig. 2.7 *Example of a stock sheet*

The stock sheet lists the number of items in stock per product line. The details of a stock check are recorded on a stock sheet before being transferred to the stock book.

No.	PRODUCT CODE	PRODUCT	STOCK LEVEL Min	STOCK LEVEL Max	Date 5/8/97 COUNTER STOCK	STOCK ROOM STOCK	TOTAL STOCK (I)	ORDER	RECEIVED	TOTAL STOCK (II)	SOLD	Date 5/8/97 COUNTER STOCK	STOCK ROOM STOCK	TOTAL STOCK (I)	ORDER	RECEIVED	TOTAL STOCK (II)	SOLD	
1	00070	Aromatic oil for vap/sc 30ml	10	14	6	2	8	2	—	8	—	6	2	8	—	2	10	—	
2	00071	Dry shampoo 250ml	6	8	3	3	6	2	—	6	2	3	1	4	2	2	6	1	
3	000072	Dry conditioner 250ml	6	8	4	4	8	—	—	8	1	3	4	7	—	—	7	—	
4	000073																		
5	00074																		
6	00075																		

Fig. 2.8 *Example of a stock book*

The stock book identifies re-order levels, and the receipt and sales of stock.

ACTIVITY

With a colleague discuss and compare your answers to the following questions:

(a) What could be the possible reasons for discrepancies at a stock check?

(b) How do you think that seasonal variations might affect the allocation of space given to stock?

(c) When are the best times for changing displays and attending to stock?

(d) Why should the salon aim for a fast turnover of stock?

(e) What sort of things should be considered when fitting out a stock room?

Computerised systems

It is possible to purchase 'off the shelf' or have individually designed computerised systems to be used in the salon or clinic reception area for appointments and stock control. Such systems will store and retrieve client information and appointment bookings. Depending on the actual programme they may give a break down of how often the client visits the clinic and what he/she spends on retail products. These packages may also store all stock control information and detail when re-ordering needs to take place. Retail products can be bar-coded for quick and easy scanning at the point of sale. Although initial setting up costs will be incurred the money spent will more than be recouped by the time saved and the efficiency of streamlining the reception and stock areas within the salon.

Fig. 2.9 *Computerised reception*

POINT TO NOTE ▷ *Computerised reception systems require a great deal of management information, e.g. the number of practitioners, rota of staff, opening hours, number of possible work areas and operational equipment etc. in order to go live. It must also be remembered that this information needs to be monitored and updated accordingly.*

Hygiene in the salon/clinic environment

It is paramount that the highest standards of hygiene are ensured within the salon to prevent infection, cross-infection and infestation, due to the close proximity of the practitioner and the client.

We spend a great deal of our lives surrounded by what are commonly known as 'germs'. Some germs are harmless, some are even beneficial, but others present a danger to us because they cause disease.

The germs which cause disease are usually spread by:

- unclean hands
- contaminated tools
- sores and pus
- discharges from the nose and mouth
- shared use of items such as towels and cups
- close contact with infected skin cells
- contaminated blood or tissue fluid.

Viruses

Viruses are the tiniest germs, yet they are responsible for an enormous range of human diseases. Viruses can only survive in living cells. The following are examples of viral infections:

- common cold: the virus is spread by coughing and sneezing and is carried through the air as a droplet infection.
- herpes simplex (cold sores): this virus remains dormant in the mucous membranes of the skin and is triggered off by sunlight or general debility. Cold sores are most likely to spread when they are weeping.
- warts: there are several types of warts. Verruca plantaris is a wart which occurs commonly under the feet and is spread by close contact.

Bacteria

Bacteria are single-celled organisms. They grow from spores and multiply very quickly. Bacteria are capable of breeding outside the body and can therefore be caught easily through personal contact or by touching a contaminated article.

Some bacteria cause diseases and infect wounds. Bacteria develop from spores which are very reproductive and highly resistant. The following are examples of bacterial infections:

- impetigo: bacteria enter the body through broken skin and cause blisters which weep and crust over. This condition is highly infectious and can be spread easily by dirty tools.

- boils: these can occur when bacteria invade the hair follicle through a surface scratch or by close contact with an infected person.
- whitlow: this can be caused by bacteria invading the pad of the finger through a break in the skin, which has often been caused by a splinter.

Fungi

Fungi consists of yeasts and moulds. Moulds break down all sorts of materials but rarely cause disease. Yeasts are single cells which can cause disease. Fungal infections are very easily transmitted by personal contact or by touching contaminated articles. The following are examples of fungal infections:

- tinea pedis (athlete's foot): in this condition the fungus thrives on the warm, moist environment between the toes and sometimes under the feet. The condition is picked up easily by direct contact with recently shed infected skin cells.
- tinea unguium (ringworm of the nail): this condition may result from contact with the fungus present on other parts of the body, e.g. toenails may become infected during an outbreak of athlete's foot, which if touched could then be spread by contact to the finger nails.

Animal parasites

Animal parasites are small insects which cause disease by invading the skin and using human blood or protein as their source of nourishment. Diseases caused by animal parasites usually occur as the result of prolonged contact with an infected person. The following are examples of diseases caused by animal parasites:

- scabies: tiny mites burrow through the outside layer of the epidermis and lay their eggs underneath the skin surface. The condition is very itchy and causes a rash and swelling. Characteristic line formations show where the burrows have been formed.
- head lice: these are small parasites which puncture the skin and suck blood. They lay eggs on the hair close to the scalp. The hatched eggs are called nits and can be seen as shiny, pearl-coloured oval bodies which cling to the hair shaft.

Protecting against disease

To protect against the spread of disease you must:

- provide each client with clean towels and gown where appropriate
- carry out a consultation before each treatment to ensure contra-indications are spotted in time
- use only tools which have been cleaned and sterilised
- where possible use disposable items, e.g. gloves, make-up brushes, tinting caps, footwear etc. use correct treatment techniques to avoid injuring the client
- dispose of waste properly after each treatment, in sharps boxes in the case of sharp objects and in properly lined bins with lids in the case of general waste
- wash your own hands before each treatment and as necessary throughout the treatment
- maintain high standards of personal hygiene.

POINT TO NOTE ▷   *Dirt and bacteria accumulate in cracks. You must not use tools with a damaged edge as they cannot be sterilised effectively.*

GOOD PRACTICE ▷

- *You have a responsibility to yourself, your clients and colleagues to always work hygienically and to do everything you can to avoid the spread of infection.*
- *All work surfaces should be cleaned regularly with hot water and detergent. The treatment couch or chair, trolley, sink and stools should be wiped down at the end of each working day with a solution of disinfectant.*
- *Waste should not be handled or exposed. Make sure that the waste resulting from your treatments is placed in a lined container, tied up and disposed of in a large sealed refuse sack with other salon waste.*

USEFUL INFORMATION

*   *Bacteria are single-celled organisms which divide in two to reproduce.*
*   *Each bacterial cell has a cell wall which offers it protection and holds it rigid.*
*   *A bacterial cell does not contain a nucleus.*

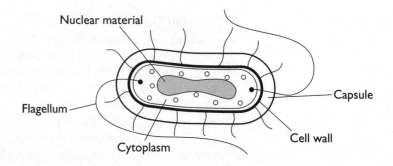

Fig. 2.10   *A typical bacterial cell*

ACTIVITY   **Research the different skin conditions affected by bacterial, viral and fungal infections. Note their names and characteristics.**

Sterilisation and disinfection

Sterilisation is the destruction of all living organisms. It is very difficult to maintain sterile conditions. Once sterilised items have been exposed to the air they are no longer sterile. Articles which have been sterilised and stored hygienically are safe to use on the client.

Autoclave

The most effective method of sterilisation is steaming at high pressure in an autoclave. This works on exactly the same principle as a pressure cooker. Steam is produced from a reservoir of water and is contained under pressure at a minimum of 121 °C for 15 minutes. Modern autoclaves have thermochromic indicators which change colour when the required temperature has been reached. Stainless steel and glass items are suitable for sterilisation by this method. A stacking facility is usually provided so that the articles can be placed at different levels in the autoclave. The very high temperature required to kill spores destroys certain materials, e.g. some plastics, in much the same way that overcooking ruins food.

Fig. 2.11 *Autoclaves*

Sanitisers

These operate by irradiating implements with ultraviolet light which would normally inactivate any bacteria. However, as all implements cannot be fully exposed directly to the ultraviolet light these units are now only recommended for storage of sterilised implements.

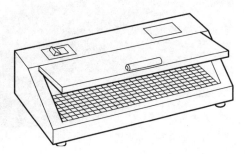

Fig. 2.12 *Sanitiser*

POINTS TO NOTE ▷
- *The ultraviolet light is at its strongest directly underneath the lamp and weaker at the front of the unit.*
- *Shaded areas of implements such as the blades of scissors would receive no exposure to the ultraviolet light.*

Glass bead sterilisers

Glass bead sterilisers reach a temperature of between 190 and 300 °C (374–572 °F) depending on the model. This temperature has to be maintained for 30–60 minutes prior to use. If extra items are put into the steriliser during this period, the temperature of the beads drops and the effects are lost. Timing has to begin again. Glass bead sterilisers can hold only very small items, e.g. tweezers, and therefore have limited use in all but the beauty therapy salon.

Chemical methods of sterilisation

Concentrated liquid chemical agents are available which have to be diluted for use. Some chemical agents act as sterilants, depending on the strength of the solution and the time for which items are kept in contact with them. Some liquid chemical sterilisers are very harmful to the skin and great care is needed when handling them.

GOOD PRACTICE ▷
You must be sure that you are carrying out safe and effective hygienic procedures. Always read and follow manufacturer's instructions carefully when preparing, using and disposing of chemical solutions.

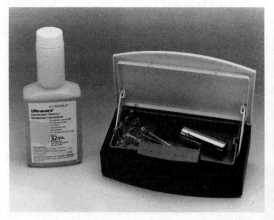 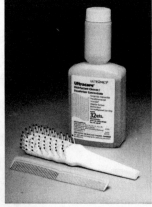

Fig. 2.13 *Ultracare sterilisation system*

Disinfection

Disinfectants work against bacteria and fungi but just remove contamination; they do not necessarily kill spores. Disinfectants only reduce the number of organisms. Examples of good chemical disinfectants are:

- gluteraldehyde: a 2% solution is used which remains active for 14–18 days, after which time it must be discarded. Gluteraldehyde is particularly useful for soaking metal instruments and applicators, but must be handled with great care. (See COSHH, Chapter 4.)
- alcohol: alcohol disinfectants have a very effective bactericidal effect. They must be used once only and then discarded.
- quartery ammonium compounds: these are bacteriostatic cleansing agents. They prevent bacteria from spreading but are not effective against very resistant organisms.
- hypochlorites: these products contain sodium or calcium hypochlorite and are often used for general cleaning purposes as they are relatively cheap. Some are corrosive and should not be used for soaking metal instruments.

GOOD PRACTICE ▷

- *Tools should always be washed in warm soapy water and rinsed well in clean water before disinfecting or sterilising them. This ensures the removal of debris which would act as a barrier. It also prevents contamination of the soaking solution.*
- *The risks of cross-infection will only be eliminated if potential disease is identified, immediate measures taken and tools and equipment are kept scrupulously clean throughout the treatment.*

POINT TO NOTE ▷   *Quartery ammonium compounds are inactivated by soap.*

Antiseptics

Antiseptics are disinfectants used specifically on the skin and for treating wounds. Ready-to-use swabs impregnated with 70% isopropyl alcohol are often used for convenience.

POINT TO NOTE ▷   *Aseptic conditions refer to creating an environment which will avoid infection.*

ACTIVITY

Research the different cleaning and sterilising methods used in two salons. Make a note of any special instructions on diluting, using and disposing of the chemical disinfectants and sterilising agents used.

KEY TERMS

You need to know what these words and phrases mean. Go back through the chapter to find out.

Salon layout
Time and motion
Choice of services
Choice of products/equipment
Retailing
Stock and stock control
Viruses
Bacteria

Fungi
Animal parasites
Sterilisation and disinfection
Autoclave
Sanitisers
Glass bead sterilisers
Antiseptics

3 Human resources (staff selection, recruitment and appraisal)

This chapter covers the following areas:
➤ establishing the needs of the business
➤ organisational structure
➤ roles, responsibilities and qualities of staff
➤ recruitment
➤ contract of employment
➤ induction
➤ appraisal
➤ staff development.

Establishing the needs of the business

Staff and their performance form the essential nucleus of a business. We are all familiar with the phrase 'you are only as good as your staff', so the recruitment, appointment, management and appraisal of all staff is paramount for a successful business.

The owner of the business must establish its actual needs before they can identify the needs of their staff. It may well be that the intention is to take over an existing business or start a new one. In this case they may wish to start small, reduce start up costs and establish a client base before leasing/purchasing premises. They may intend to operate a mobile/home visiting service or even set up a room either in their home or rent a work area within an existing or new business. Once the decision has been made to either take over and develop an existing business, expand from a 'one man band' size business or establish a large business, a lot of thought must be given to the staff needs including, over a three-year time span, the organisational structure, roles of staff and the numbers required. This ensures that staff time and skills are maximised to acknowledge the demands of the growing business, and therefore increases the viability and potential of the business.

Many practitioners within the health, beauty and hairdressing industries start their career within their chosen profession as employees, thus enabling them to increase their knowledge, skills and business awareness of their particular industry. It is an ideal way for an enthusiastic career-minded practitioner to learn the business, observing its strengths and weakness and building up a wealth of knowledge that can one day be called upon. It is often more difficult for holistic practitioners such as acupuncturists, chiropractors, trichologists etc. as the present business climate tends to lead them towards self-employment once they are qualified. However, many holistic practitioners often hire rooms within clinics affording them the opportunity to share experience, knowledge and problems with others; this can be a great learning curve for such practitioners. The opportunity may arise for one of them to establish their own clinic either recruiting staff, or hiring out rooms or space to other practitioners, and it must always be remembered that a wide variety of experience is extremely beneficial to any health, beauty or hairdressing business.

Organisational structure

The organisational structure of the business will obviously be dependent on a number of factors, i.e. the size of the business, the role and personal view of the owner or owners and financial constraints.

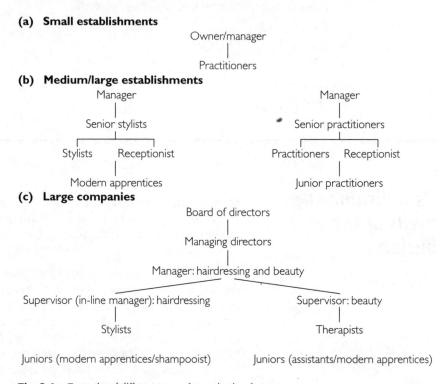

(a) Small establishments

Owner/manager
|
Practitioners

(b) Medium/large establishments

Manager   Manager
| |
Senior stylists   Senior practitioners

Stylists   Receptionist   Practitioners   Receptionist
| |
Modern apprentices   Junior practitioners

(c) Large companies

Board of directors
|
Managing directors
|
Manager: hairdressing and beauty

Supervisor (in-line manager): hairdressing   Supervisor: beauty
| |
Stylists   Therapists

Juniors (modern apprentices/shampooist)   Juniors (assistants/modern apprentices)

Fig. 3.1 *Examples of different types of organisational structures*

In the case of sole traders the organisational structure will not be relevant; however, it is important to consider when drawing up a five-year plan the possible growth of the business and its future recruitment. It must also be noted that many sole traders intend from the onset of their business to establish a good client base and remain totally self-employed. Many successful businesses operate like this and in any industry providing there is a need there will always be a market.

POINT TO NOTE ▷   A *well-structured organisational system ensures efficient flow of communication within the business.*

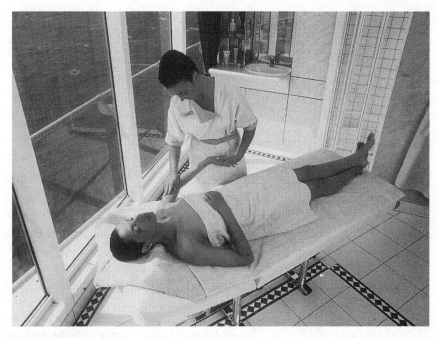

Fig. 3.2 *Salon at sea*

Roles, responsibilities and qualities of staff

In order to consider an organisational flow chart to suit the business the owner must firstly understand the roles of different personnel.

Roles and responsibilities of the employer

The employer has overall control of the well-being and efficient running of the business whether or not they are directly involved in it. In some cases the owner may decide to leave total management of the business to an employee or board of employees or shareholders. This is often dependent on the size of the business or the knowledge and or time constraints of the owner.

Role and responsibilities of the manager

All businesses need a leader, this may be the owner, director or manager. Managerial success is often judged on a person's ability to lead, however it is hard to actually define leadership especially as modern businesses tend to need a degree of democracy to help create a consensus on the aims and objectives of the business. It is one of the manager's roles to encourage ambition through a desire to contribute to the success of the business.

Some important qualities of a leader

A good leader:

- provides a positive sense of direction
- prepares for tomorrow's problems today
- thinks clearly and rationally
- uses initiative
- creates an enthusiastic atmosphere

- adapts to change
- creates a sense of value and purpose in work
- acts decisively
- is sensitive to staff needs
- evaluates what motivates individuals
- builds on people's strengths.

These qualities will ensue that the manager is able to undertake the roles required to run the business effectively, i.e.:

- to present a clear, logical business plan
- to implement, monitor and review the business plan
- to train, direct, co-ordinate, counsel and appraise employees
- to delegate responsibility as appropriate
- to be a proactive manager who is able to be reactive if required.

POINTS TO NOTE ▷ *Proactive is used to describe a style of management whereby the manager analyses and prepares for the future business needs and possible crises.*

Reactive is used to describe a style of management whereby the manager reacts to situations as they occur.

In small establishments the role of the manager may be performed by the employer. It is not an easy task as it requires a great deal of skill and judgment. The personal qualities that make a good manager are:

- enthusiasm about the business and the industry in general. It is essential that they have wide ranging experience of the industry particularly if they are managing a diverse practice, e.g. hairdressing and beauty salon, natural health clinic etc. It is not essential that they have personal experience across all the treatments offered but they should have an understanding of these enabling them to build a global picture of the services, their importance and relevance to the business to ensure it meets current and future demands.
- willingness to listen and learn. The ability to listen is paramount when working with others. The manager will need to listen and learn from staff, clients and other professionals to enable them to manage the business successfully.
- the ability to juggle many tasks at the same time. Working in a service industry requires the manager to deal and liaise with clients and staff to ensure its smooth operation. This may include in a small business book keeping, wages, stock control, marketing and promotion etc.
- patience and tact. It is necessary when dealing with staff and clients' problems, both on a business and a personal level, to be extremely patient and diplomatic.
- knowledge of new trends. With rapid growth in technology and growing client awareness of health and fitness it is essential that the manager keeps abreast of changes within their industry. This may be through a variety of routes, e.g. membership of a professional association,

attending exhibitions, conferences, seminars, reading current journals and new text books etc.

- excellent personal and interpersonal skills. The life force of a service industry is its ability to understand and communicate with its clients, therefore when managing this type of business it is paramount that the manager exudes the skills of tact and diplomacy. They must be able to communicate with and motivate their staff, be punctual and of immaculate appearance thus setting an example for staff to emulate.

Qualities to look for in employees

Personal and interpersonal skills

These skills are often referred to by different names, e.g. life skills, key skills, core skills, social skills, but are seen as an essential quality for anyone working within a service industry and include skills such as communication, listening, working as a member of a team, personal presentation, organisational skills/time management, numeracy, literacy and information technology.

Communication

Every day we communicate with our family, friends and colleagues in a variety of ways, e.g. conversation, telephone, facsimile, letter writing, memos, reports, interviewing, body language etc. Over the past decade technology has advanced enormously and many business will have a variety of electronic equipment to assist in communication procedures. All businesses tend to have a telephone and others have additional 'gadgets' such as answer phones and fax machines. Some may also have mobile phones, E-mail and access to the Internet.

Communication can be broken down into two main types:

Verbal   The use of oral communication

Non-verbal   The use of non-oral communication

ACTIVITY

1 Categorise each of the following under Verbal or Non-verbal Communication:

   (a) telephone call

   (b) fax message

   (c) letter

   (d) smile

   (e) appointment card

   (f) hand shake

   (g) frown

   (h) folded arms.

2 (a) Give three examples of friendly body language.

   (b) Give three examples of uninterested body language signs.

3 Describe the psychological effect on a client who is greeted with signs of uninterested body language.

4 State the advantages and disadvantages of using verbal and non-verbal methods of communication.

Listening skills

One of the main benefits to clients of health, beauty and hairdressing establishments is the release of stress often brought about through the 'off loading' of problems or concerns they might have. Quite often they are seeking reassurance that these concerns whether about the way they look or feel are relevant to their age group. The practitioner must learn to listen to and be receptive to the client, to analyse and identify their needs and provide the relevant service. This may be the actual treatment, e.g. style or colour of hair or make-up etc. It is important to remember to listen and not get personally involved. Only offer advice and guidance if it is within your qualifications to do so, e.g. professional counselling.

Many clients prefer the maturity of older practitioners who have learnt to develop these listening skills and provide the client with the correct level of empathy, support, respect and identity.

Working as a member of a team

In any business which involves more than one person, team work is important. It is essential that practitioners are able to use their initiative and not await instruction on tasks that would be considered to be common sense, e.g.:

- cleaning and tidying up after others to ensure the establishment remains in pristine condition and appearance
- helping another practitioner to prepare for a client
- assisting with the reception area
- taking care of waiting clients
- cleaning and tidying the staff and stock room
- washing up dirty glasses and cups immediately after client's use.

Team work is not a natural ability that everyone possess as some people just do not function easily as part of a team and are more suited to working on their own. However, if a person has good interpersonal skills the owner or manager can assist them in developing and building this skill in order to maximise the business potential. Some people just need more support and confidence-building to work effectively as team members.

Personal presentation

In a service industry personal presentation is paramount. Close contact with others means the practitioner must have impeccable personal hygiene. Often things that are considered common sense to some are not obvious to others, e.g.:

- washing daily (more often if the individual has a problem with perspiration)
- using deodorants
- wearing clean well-laundered clothing suitable for the work place. The business may well have a set uniform or colour scheme
- wearing clean suitable shoes in accordance with the regulations of the business

- ensuring hair is clean, presentable and styled in accordance with any regulations (it may be that the business expects the practitioner to neatly tie back long hair)

- cleaning teeth after eating foods with a strong odour, and after smoking

- washing hands after using the toilet, smoking, handling foods or stock with strong odours and prior to treating a client. It may also be necessary during the treatment time to re-wash hands, i.e. after blowing one's nose, coughing into one's hands or as part of treatment procedure, such as in beauty prior to and after extraction, or in hairdressing and beauty after handling or removing products

- maximising the individual's appearance to reflect the type of business, e.g. a hairdressing salon will generally want its staff to reflect current trends in cuts, perms and colours to suit the employees' personality and age range. A salon specialising in aromatherapy etc. will generally expect its therapists to have short unvarnished nails with a suitable uniform to allow for ease of movement. A nail salon will expect the technicians to have beautifully manicured nails.

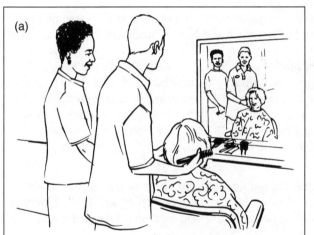
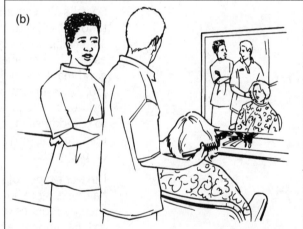

Fig. 3.3 (**a**) and (**c**) show examples of good practice in non-verbal communication; (**b**) and (**d**) show examples of poor practice.

GOOD PRACTICE ▷

- *Include a business personal presentation regulation leaflet (stating guidelines for suitable attire for dress, presentation of hair and nails and hygiene reminders) as part of staff induction. Display this leaflet in a prominent position for staff to see and remind them of its existence.*
- *Ensure each staff member has a locker for storage of mouth fresheners, toothpaste and brush, spare uniform and deodorant etc.*

ACTIVITY

Draw up suitable personal presentation guidelines for:

(a) a beauty therapist

(b) an aromatherapist or reflexologist

(c) a homeopath, a herbalist or an iridologist

(d) an acupuncturist or a chiropractor

(e) a hairdresser.

Social skills

Social skills encompass communication, listening and personal presentation along with the ability to act and behave appropriately. These skills are invaluable as clients will feel relaxed, happy and content in an establishment where all the staff display consistent high standards of good manners, politeness, empathy, enthusiasm and happiness with their job, environment and colleagues. It is important to establish quickly the individual's behavioural needs in terms of the manner in which they wish to be addressed, e.g. Mr/Mrs/Miss/Dr etc., and treated, e.g. allowed to read, talk or sit quietly and the support they need, e.g. encouragement, empathy etc.

Different types of jobs will require different types of personalities, e.g. hairdressing requires an outgoing personality with an artistic flair, beauty therapy requires a caring nature with good listening skills and a well-groomed appearance.

ACTIVITY

Explain how you would handle each of the following clients:

(a) middle-aged women with low self esteem

(b) thirty-eight year old male concerned over his loss of hair

(c) fifty year old woman who has lost confidence in her role as all her children have left home

(d) twenty year old women suffering from pre-menstrual tension

(e) forty year old recently divorced male who is lonely

(f) thirty year old business woman suffering from work-related stress

(g) twenty-five year old female buying her first home and suffering from stress

(h) eighteen year old male whose mother has recently died and is depressed

(i) forty-five year old male suffering from insomnia.

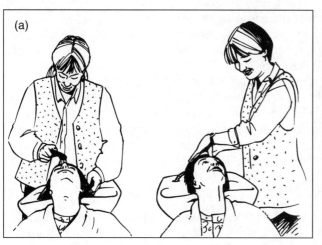
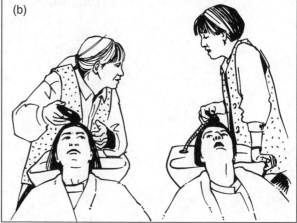

Fig. 3.4 *Examples of (**a**) good and (**b**) poor standards in client care*

GOOD PRACTICE ▷ *It is useful to gently encourage clients with stress-related problems or low self esteem to:*

- *find someone with whom they can discuss their problem, fears and worries*
- *keep healthy through diet and exercise*
- *develop new hobbies or interests and friends*
- *find time to relax.*

POINTS TO NOTE ▷ **Key qualities of a hair stylist**
Professional qualifications
Personal/interpersonal skills – outgoing personality, able to relate to all clients
Social skills
Energy and enthusiasm
Artistic flair
Fashionable appearance and dress sense

Key qualities of a beauty therapist
Professional qualifications
Personal/interpersonal skills – caring nature, able to listen to and relate to all
 clients
Social skills
Energy and enthusiasm
Well-groomed appearance

Key qualities of a holistic practitioner
Professional qualifications
Personal/interpersonal skills – mature, caring nature, able to listen and analyse
Social skills
Energy and enthusiasm
Professional appearance and manner

Organisational skills/time management

The way in which employees manage themselves and their time is crucial to the business. Some people are born organisers and can quickly adapt to the needs of the business whereas others need guidance and support and some have no understanding of this at all. Time is of the essence when working in either health, beauty or hairdressing as appointments revolve around time. A practitioner has to make the most of the time between treatments to prepare both physically and emotionally for the next client. When launching new treatments or marketing them consideration has to be given to time, i.e. time needed to perform the treatments, time for staff training, suitability of the treatment to the time of year, e.g. slimming treatments after Christmas and before holidays.

Punctuality is an essential requirement when employing a person to work within the service industry. It is essential that all employees are aware that if clients are booked in from 9.00 a.m. they will need to be in work prior to this in order to prepare for the treatment. Throughout the day practitioners have to work to time constraints as clients will not be prepared to continually wait five, ten or fifteen minutes later than their scheduled appointment. If this continually happens they are more than likely to go elsewhere.

ACTIVITY

Carry out a time and motion study of a local business taking into account the position of equipment, products, treatment areas, staff room, storage area etc.

GOOD PRACTICE ▷

- To assist staff in maximising their time it is useful to carry out a time and motion study.
- Involve staff in a time and motion study of their working areas to ensure they maximise the use of their time.
- It is useful to prepare a list of clients for each practitioner for the whole day so that they can prepare in advance and best utilise their time.

Numeracy/literacy

It is essential that all practitioners have basic literacy and numeracy skills in order to be able to communicate and handle money within the business, e.g. record appointments, take messages, handle stock, record, receive and maintain accurate financial transactions etc.

Information technology (IT)

In today's modern world computer literacy is a compulsory part of the school curriculum. Many businesses have a computer for word processing and some are introducing computerised systems to record appointments and accounts. IT skills are extremely useful and can be used as a professional mechanism for communicating, i.e. word processing skills being used for letter and memo writing, promotional notices, newsletters etc. and design skills being used to produce promotional leaflets, price lists etc. It is important for an employee to highlight their skills in this area as if they are utilised they could save the business time and money.

POINT TO NOTE ▷ *Recent media reports in the United Kingdom have highlighted growing concern amongst employers over the growing shortage of skilled workers and in particular those with good personal/interpersonal skills.*

The role and responsibilities of the practitioner

It goes without saying that all practitioners should be well trained and qualified. They need to be enthusiastic about their work with a willingness to learn and develop skills. They need to have a flexible approach and be happy to work as a member of a team adapting their roles to assist colleagues and the ultimate success of the business. Excellent personal, interpersonal and life skills are an essential requirement when working with the public.

In order to ensure that staff have reputable qualifications the manager, if not a specialist in this particular skill area, may need to investigate recognised qualifications through organisations such as professional associations, national training organisations or industry lead bodies. This may be necessary for the owner or manager of a hair and beauty salon who by trade is a qualified hairdresser and needs to recruit a beauty therapist, or for the chiropractor opening a clinic and wishing to employ other practitioners such as a reflexologist, aromatherapist, homeopath and acupuncturist. It is not sufficient for the manager just to take the advice of an employee or friend as they can often only draw on their own experience and knowledge. It may be that the potential employee qualified five yeas ago and training and qualifications may have changed due to government and or examining or awarding body policies. When employing people for a particular skill it is essential to contact the specialists within that trade if the business is to recruit the right person for the job.

The role and responsibilities of the receptionist

The receptionist is the first point of contact that a client has with the business and therefore has an extremely important role. The reception area may be staffed by more than one person in larger establishments and by the practitioners themselves in smaller concerns. It is therefore essential that all those working in reception have a thorough under-standing of the workings of the business and are extremely professional in their approach and appearance. It is also beneficial for them to have an understanding of the benefits of the treatments and retail products on offer within the establishment. Whoever performs the task of receptionist needs to be well trained in the workings of the reception area as potential business can be lost through incompetence.

Fig. 3.5 *Examples of (**a**) good and (**b**) poor reception skills*

POINTS TO NOTE ▷ *The reception area is the life line of the business. It is here that:*

- *the appointment book is kept; this is the central control of the business, everybody plans their activities for the day around this*
- *appointments are made either by telephone or by clients in person*
- *clients are greeted and made welcome by the receptionist*
- *clients and visitors to the salon, e.g. cosmetic/hairdressing company representatives, are taken care of whilst waiting. However, it is extremely important that staff do not discuss any business matters in an area where clients may overhear financial purchasing arrangements etc.*
- *enquiries are dealt with, e.g. information on salon treatments, products, planned salon events, directions to another shop in the area*
- *products are ordered, received, recorded, priced, displayed and sold*
- *services offered within the business are advertised*
- *payment is taken for treatments and retail products.*

All of the tasks outlined above are generally undertaken by the receptionist, whose job mainly involves taking, receiving and recording information either by telephone or in person.

GOOD PRACTICE ▷ *In order for a receptionist to deal either with clients or visitors to the business they need to fully understand the workings of the establishment including the:*

- *roles and responsibilities of each member of staff*
- *recording mechanisms used (manual or computer-operated systems)*
- *treatments offered and their benefits*
- *retail products sold.*

Fig. 3.6 *Consultation area*

The receptionist must remain courteous to all clients and visitors and treat them all as equals. Generally clients are polite and friendly; however, some people can demand a great deal of attention and at times can be aggressive and rude. The receptionist must stay cool, calm and collected, as they represent the business and as the first point of contact will create an impression of the business to the client or visitor. A friendly smile and voice can often help to dissipate the aggression of a visitor. Everybody experiences bad days but when working in a service industry individuals' moods have to be left at home. However, clients and visitors may not always manage to do this so its important that receptionists are made aware and reminded that they are probably just an outlet for the client or visitor's emotions; it is highly probable that it is not personal and should not be taken as such.

POINT TO NOTE ▷ *Behaviour breeds behaviour. Remember the last time your brother or sister shouted at you? You probably shouted back; next time try smiling and responding in a quiet calm voice until they are softened by your behaviour.*

Telephone enquiries

For many clients the telephone is their main point of contact with the business. A good receptionist never forgets that all calls are from existing or prospective clients.

GOOD PRACTICE ▷

- Answer promptly – between the second and fourth ring. This gives both the caller and the receptionist time to prepare themselves without the caller becoming impatient.
- Be friendly – give the name of the business and your name. Make a note of the client's name so that you can use it during the conversation.
- Smile when you pick up the receiver. Your voice is you to a caller. Smiles definitely do travel down the telephone!
- Be enthusiastic – ask how you may help the caller. Remember that enthusiasm is infectious and shows the caller that you enjoy being helpful.
- Listen attentively – it is very off-putting for a caller if they sense that the receptionist is being distracted by someone else.
- Leave a good impression. Remember that as the receptionist you represent the business to the caller. Make sure you repeat back to them any important points that have been discussed and thank them for calling. Don't forget to use the clients name throughout the conversation.

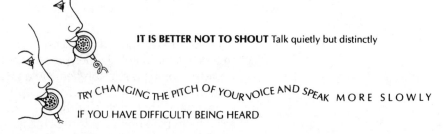

IT IS BETTER NOT TO SHOUT Talk quietly but distinctly

TRY CHANGING THE PITCH OF YOUR VOICE AND SPEAK MORE SLOWLY IF YOU HAVE DIFFICULTY BEING HEARD

Fig. 3.7   Tips for using the telephone

POINTS TO NOTE ▷

- The telephone is for business use and should not be used for chatty personal calls. Clients who cannot get through may give up and make an appointment somewhere else.
- It is a good idea to have a telephone answering machine. This records messages outside business hours and is particularly useful for clients to use in the event of a cancellation.

Taking messages

It is essential that all messages are accurately recorded and promptly dealt with. The receptionist must record who the message is for, who it is from, the telephone number where they can be contacted, the date and time of the message, the actual message and state whether they want their call returned, will call again or were returning a call. The person taking the message should also record their name in case there are any queries. An example of a message recording sheet is shown in Fig. 3.8.

To: Date:

From: Time:

Tel. no.:   Taken by:

Message:

Please return their call

Will call again

Returning your call

MAKE SURE ALL INFORMATION IS CLEARLY RECORDED AND PASSED ON PROMPTLY.

Fig. 3.8 *Message recording sheet*

Recording appointments

This is an extremely important part of the receptionist's job and it is essential that all staff understand the appointment system in operation. Appointment sheets must always be made up in advance, thus enabling clients to book courses of treatments and to assist them with planning in advance.

GOOD PRACTICE ▷

- *Ensure that the reception desk is supplied with appointment cards, pens, pencils, ruler and rubber.*
- *Prepare the pages in the appointment book at least eight weeks in advance, to show the availability of each practitioner on a particular day.*
- *As appointments are arranged, transfer the details to the appointment book in pencil, stating the client's name, their telephone number and the treatment required.*
- *Make out an appointment card for the client, recording the details in pen, stating the date, day, time, treatment and practitioner's name.*
- *Check the accuracy of both sets of records before handing over the appointment card to the client.*
- *Record the client's arrival at the salon by drawing a diagonal line in pencil across their details in the appointment book.*
- *When the client has gone through for treatment, draw a second diagonal line across the first one to record that they are being attended to.*
- *Clients who arrive unexpectedly may be treated provided that there is a practitioner available. The receptionist should always check first and then record the client's details on the day in the appointment book.*
- *In some establishments the receptionist prepares a list for each practitioner which shows their schedule for the day. This is kept by the practitioner and provides a useful quick reference to assist them in planning for the day*

DATE: Monday 19th January 1998		THE HAIR AND BEAUTY COMPANY		
	STYLIST JULIE	STYLIST JEAN	SENIOR APPRENTICE RACHEL	LEIGH	BEAUTY THERAPIST KIM
8.30					
8.45					
9.00	Mr Mernagh	Mrs Lees SIS	Mrs Perry		Helene DNA
9.15	CBD 224 7761	Mrs Dainty	Highlights	MORNING	Emma EP C
9.30	Mrs Peet	CBD 7947772		OFF	Ms Fisher
9.45	CBD 143 9800	Mrs Godfrey	NC		Man Bridal
10.00	Mr Lloyd	CBD	787 1234		M up
10.15	CBD 333 4444	Mrs Perry			999 6644
10.30	Ms Fisher	CBD NC	Mrs Turvey		Jennie C.
10.45	BRIDE	Liz Cogin	Colour		Facial
11.00		CBD	292 2929		
11.15	999 6644	Turvey			7152244
11.30	Mrs Robinson	CBD			Mrs Wensley
11.45	Long hair perm	Emma Merris			Ped
12.00	299 8211				700 1000
12.15		Long hair			
12.30	LUNCH	246 7891	LUNCH		LUNCH
12.45				Ken	
13.00	Mrs	LUNCH		CBD	
13.15	Robinson		M. Severn	Mrs Bryan	Val Cooke
13.30	CBD		HL	CBD	Facial
13.45	Andrew Lloyd	D. Bona C	NC	Mrs Lynch	
14.00	CBD 533 1944	BD 888 1818	987 6453	CBD	642 1357
14.15	Liz Lloyd	M. Severn CBD NC		Mrs Daly	Mrs Slattery
14.30	CBD	987 6543		Perm 345 2817	Man 400 4000

☐	Available Time		⊠	Client has been taken for treatment
◹	Client arrived and is awaiting treatment		DNA	Did not attend – client did not inform: make a note on record card
NC	New client		C	Last minute cancellation

Fig. 3.9(a) *Completed page of a hair and beauty salon appointment book*

GOOD PRACTICE ▷

- It is important that the appointment pages are kept neat and tidy. The correct codes and abbreviations must be used and the start and finish times of treatments made clear.
- Sometimes clients have to cancel or change their appointment. When details are recorded in pencil, they can be rubbed out neatly and the space used for another client.

DATE: Monday 9th February 1998 — THE NATURAL HEALTH CARE CLINIC

	AROMATHERAPY EVE	SPORT MASSAGE JUNE	REFLEXOLOGY MITCH	ACUPUNCTURE DEAN	McTIMONEY CHIROPRACTOR AARTI
8.30					
8.45					
9.00					D. Williams
9.15					091 2229
9.30	Sasha			Mr S. James	Mrs Mernagh
9.45	Lill	MORNING			579 9229
10.00	NC	OFF			R. Rees
10.15			Moira		
10.30	808 9090		Paulusz	NC	NC
10.45				100 1000	478 2919
11.00	Marion		NC		J. Pope
11.15	Cornford		217 9229		987 9293
11.30				Laurence	Heidi
11.45	DNA		Kisa	Green	189 7993
12.00	595 7279		C Osborne		Lorraine Walker
12.15					552 5651
12.30	LUNCH		NC	877 7788	Bob Reeve
12.45			550 4143		
13.00	Mrs	Ian			NC
13.15	Koncevicius	Archibold	LUNCH	LUNCH	877 7788
13.30					
13.45	NC	335 3939	Kate	John	LUNCH
14.00			Jenkins	M.	
14.15	707 8090		712 7679		
14.30				243 2434	Adam

☐	Available Time	⊠	Client has been taken for treatment
◰	Client arrived and is awaiting treatment	DNA	Did not attend – client did not inform: make a note on record card
NC	New client	C	Last minute cancellation

Fig. 3.9(b)   *Completed page of a natural health clinic appointment book*

Support staff

In larger establishments roles such as cleaning, laundry, handling of stock, preparation of working areas etc. may be performed by support staff which will obviously add to the overall efficiency of services provided. It is important that everyone in the establishment can deal with these areas if continuity is to be maintained, e.g. in a busy hairdressing salon a shampooist may be employed to prepare the client and perform other such duties to assist in the smooth running of the salon but if the shampooist is off sick everyone needs to help out.

Recruitment

At some time it may be necessary to recruit staff, either for a new business, an expanding business or to replace staff who have left the business. It is essential that the owner firstly establishes that the position is needed. Perhaps the vacancy has occurred as someone is leaving for another job or because they are moving home and it is not feasible for them to remain in the job, or it may be a female who is taking maternity leave. It is important for the owner to ask themselves:

- Do I need to replace this member of staff?
- Are we under-staffed?
- Is there a need now or in the near future for this skill area?

Consideration must also be given when recruiting new staff to ensure there is a need within the business for additional skills that existing staff can not offer.

Once the owner has established that there is a need to recruit staff it is essential to establish whether the position requires full or part-time employment as well as the role and skills needed. The owner or manager must then investigate the qualifications needed for that skill area, the investment required in terms of space, equipment, materials etc., the potential increase in turnover and then outline the job description which will give a clear definition of the actual job along with the responsibilities it includes. The salary to be offered should be determined and an advertisement drawn up stating the title of the job, the name of the business, the job specification or requirements, the hours required to cover the businesses needs, the salary, who the point of contact will be for enquiries and the deadline set for applications.

Title of the job	Full time beauty therapist
Name of the salon	Complexion Beauty Salon, London
Specification	Beauty therapist needed to provide facial, body and epilation treatments and to work as part of a team
Location	Within a busy city centre salon
Hours	37 hours per week with one late night
Salary	£10 000 per annum plus commission
Contact	For application forms contact Miss Fisher on 0171 100 1000
Deadline	Applications open until Friday 18th July 1997

Fig. 3.10(a) *Example of a job advertisement for a beauty therapist*

Title of the job	Hair stylist
Name of the salon	The Hair Company, Birmingham
Specification	Experienced hair stylist needed to work as part of a team
Location	Within a busy city centre salon
Hours	37 hours per week with one late night
Salary	£9000 per annum plus commission
Contact	for application forms contact Mrs Horton on 0121 100 1000
Deadline	Applications open until Friday 16th May 1997

Fig. 3.10(b) *Example of a job advertisement for a hair stylist*

Setting the standards of the business

Standards required by applicants will vary according to the role, i.e. the specification for a hairdressing junior in a small suburban salon will be different to that for a stylist or even manager in a city salon for a large company with many salons throughout the country, just as the specifications for a manager or receptionist in a health clinic will also vary. There are, however, certain factors that the person drawing up the job specification must consider and these are:

1 What are the standards of the skill area involved?
These may be broken down into either specific skill areas, e.g.:

In *beauty*:

Body treatments,

Facial treatments

Epilation treatments

or

Manual treatments

Electrotherapy treatments

or

Individual treatments

In *hairdressing*:

Perming

Colouring

Cutting

In *health clinics*:

Chiropractors

Aromatherapy

Reflexology etc.

The standards for these skills are very important to ensure an excellent standard of treatments is maintained by all practitioners throughout the business.

2 What are the standards required on appearance?
This covers the appearance of the staff, e.g. personal hygiene and dress, which will reflect the image of the business, and the appearance of the business premises, e.g. hygiene, tidiness, decor and display material, which reflects the image of the salon.

3 What are the standards of staff behaviour?
How the staff respond to clients and colleagues alike will help create the atmosphere within the salon and therefore standards must be set.

4 What are the standards on the general service to clients?
The required standard for greeting and taking care of the client in the reception area is important to establish and should include guidance on the treatments and retail products offered by the business.

5 What are the targets on productivity?
Standards must be set for guidance on treatment times, retail and service targets as well as utilising business time to its maximum.

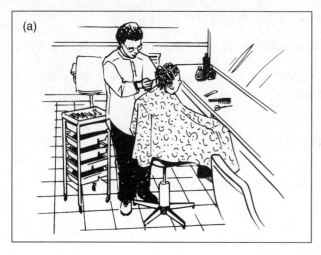

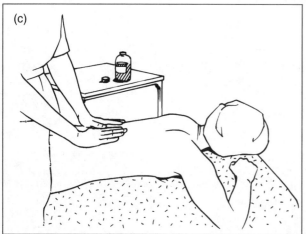
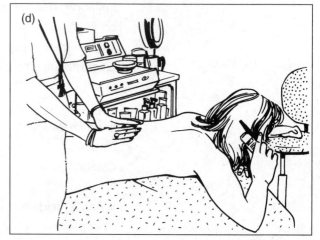

Fig. 3.11 (*a*) *and* (*c*) *show examples of good standards in skills, behaviour and health and safety;* (*b*) *and* (*d*) *show examples of poor standards*

Recruitment routes

It is important when recruiting staff to consider the various routes available such as:

- advertising in a local newspaper
- advertising in a national trade journal
- advertising in a professional association newsletter
- contacting training colleges
- contacting a recruitment agency
- making enquiries through business colleagues etc.
- internal applicants seeking promotion.

POINT TO NOTE ▷   *Ensure your job recruitment advertisement does not break any current legislation, e.g. the Equal Opportunities Act.*

Health & Beauty Salon   79

***Fig.* 3.12**   *Trade journal recruitment page*

51

Steiner STEINER TRAINING PLACEMENT COURSE
– APPLICATION FORM

FULL NAME:	ATTACH
DATE OF BIRTH:	2 ×
PLEASE STATE WHERE YOU HEARD ABOUT WORKING ON A CRUISE SHIP:	PASSPORT
	PHOTOS
A. STEINER REP. VISITING YOUR COLLEGE	HERE

B. ADVERT: PLEASE STATE MAGAZINE/NEWSPAPER

C. TRADE EXHIBITION: PLEASE STATE WHICH ONE

D. THROUGH A FRIEND

E. OTHER

APPLYING FOR POSITION OF: BEAUTY THERAPIST ☐ MASSAGE THERAPIST ☐

HAIR STYLIST ☐ NURSE ☐ RECEPTIONIST ☐ CHIROPODIST ☐

FITNESS/AEROBIC INSTRUCTOR ☐ NAIL TECHNICIAN ☐

IF YOU ARE A STUDENT, PLEASE SPECIFY WHAT SUBJECT YOU ARE CURRENTLY STUDYING AND THE DATE YOU WILL GRADUATE

SUBJECT	DATE

HOME ADDRESS:

COUNTY:	POST CODE:	COUNTRY:

TEL: (DAY)	TEL: (EVE)

NEXT OF KIN NAME:	RELATIONSHIP:
ADDRESS:	

COUNTY:	POST CODE:	TEL:

NATIONALITY:	PLACE OF BIRTH:

PLEASE DELETE: SINGLE/MARRIED/DIVORCED/SEPARATED/	NO. OF CHILDREN:

AGE OF CHILDREN:	HEIGHT:	WEIGHT:	SEX:

DRESS SIZE (FEMALES):	DO YOU HOLD A BRITISH PASSPORT?:

IF NOT, PLEASE SPECIFY FROM WHICH COUNTRY:

PASSPORT NO:	DATE OF ISSUE:

PLACE OF ISSUE:	EXPIRY DATE:

DO YOU HAVE A WORK PERMIT FOR 1. UNITED KINGDOM OR 2. UNITED STATES?

1. U.K.: YES/NO EXPIRY DATE:	2. U.S.A.: YES/NO EXPIRY DATE:

Fig. 3.13   *Example of a job application form*

Steiner TRAINING

NAME OF COLLEGE/SALON	DATES ATTENDED	EXAMINATIONS PASSED WITH GRADES

ADDITIONAL COURSES TAKEN

EMPLOYMENT RECORD

EMPLOYER NAME, ADDRESS & TELEPHONE NO.:
1)
2)
3)
4)

POSITION HELD	DATES OF EMPLOYMENT	REASONS FOR LEAVING
1)	1)	1)
2)	2)	2)
3)	3)	3)
4)	4)	4)

PROVIDE NAME, ADDRESS & TELEPHONE NO. OF 2 REFERENCES OF EMPLOYER AND/OR COLLEGE TUTOR

1)
2)

MEDICAL HISTORY	
DO YOU SUFFER FROM ANY DISABILITY/SERIOUS ILLNESS (INCL. R.S.I.)?	YES / NO
PLEASE GIVE DETAILS	
CAN YOU SWIM?:	
INCLUDING YOUR NATIVE TONGUE, WHAT LANGUAGES DO YOU SPEAK AND TO WHAT	
LEVEL?:	

Fig. 3.13 _Example of a job application form (continued)_

It is important for any business to recruit the best person for the job so it is therefore essential that as wide a field as possible will apply for the position. The owner needs to be prepared for enquiries and, depending on the size of the business, may have their own standard application forms. Application forms will generally request information on the applicant such as: name, address, telephone number, date of birth, gender, secondary school qualifications (GCSEs, GNVQs, A-levels etc.), vocational training and qualifications (NVQs, CIBTAC, C + G etc.), previous and present employment history and salary along with a section for additional information such as special awards, social interests etc.

It is important for employers to keep abreast of educational changes in order to ensure that they do not disregard or discredit a prospective employee's qualifications. Education systems are reviewed and amended, just as an employer reviews and upgrades their business, and it is therefore highly likely that at some time they may come across an educational or vocational qualification that is different to their own. In recent years the education system in the United Kingdom has seen great changes in terms of the mechanisms used to measure outputs such as the introduction of assessment as well as/or in place of final examinations. The content or subject matter studied will also have altered to keep abreast of changes in consumer requirements, technological advancements etc.

POINT TO NOTE ▷ *If the decision has been made to take over an existing business such as a hairdressing or beauty salon then by law the new owner is obliged to take on the existing staff.*

Job descriptions

A job description needs to be prepared in advance so that it can be forwarded to anyone requesting information on the vacant position from the advertisement etc. It should state the following:

- job title and position
- location
- position of person the job holder will be responsible to
- number of staff, if any, the job holder will be responsible for
- main purpose of the job
- tasks involved in the job
- any special requirements of the job, e.g. travel, late nights, equipment the job holder may have to supply etc.
- salary
- hours of work
- holiday entitlement.

Title	Hair and beauty manager
Location	The Hair Company, 44 Main Road, Manchester
Responsible to	The proprietor
No. of staff	Responsible for a team of three beauty therapists, three stylists, one junior and two part-time receptionists.
Purpose	Responsible for the efficient operation and financial management of the salon. Ensuring that the high standards of the company are maintained by all staff.
Tasks	• To monitor and review the needs of the salon.
	• To maintain high standards of service within the salon.
	• To monitor, review and assess staff training needs in line with the potential growth of the business.
	• To maintain the company's policies on personal appearance, salon hygiene, time keeping and discipline.
	• To maintain accurate accounts and book keeping systems.
	• To maintain clear records for stock control.
	• To achieve set quarterly targets.
	• To establish training programmes to meet the staff and future salon needs.
	• To encourage and motivate all staff.
	• To draw up job specifications as required, advertise, interview recruit and carry out induction/training programmes.

Fig. 3.14 *Example of a job description*

GOOD PRACTICE ▷

- *In order to maximise staff potential it is essential to ensure that each staff member has a job description and is fully aware of what their individual job actually involves. Job descriptions also serve as a vehicle for monitoring staff progress, disciplining staff, training staff, motivating staff and appraising staff.*
- *Most job descriptions will include an open-ended statement allowing the employer to add in duties from time to time as they see fit.*

ACTIVITY

Draft a suitable advertisement for a local paper and a clear structured job description (where appropriate) for each of the following:

(a) manager of a large city centre hairdressing and beauty salon

(b) aromatherapist for a suburban health clinic

(c) room to let two days a week within a health clinic for an acupuncturist

(d) apprentice hairdresser for a small village salon.

Preparing to select applicants for interview

It is always useful to draw up a short listing form ensuring that there is space to list the applicants' names along with essential and desirable requirements (see the examples in Fig. 3.15). However, before this can be prepared it is necessary to list what are considered to be the essential and what are the desirable or preferable qualifications and attributes needed for the job.

						Interviewee's name		Job title – stylist
						C+G NVQ LEVEL II/C+G 300–01 HAIRDRESSING	Essential attributes	
						Good level of personal presentation		
						Clear voice		
						Pleasant manner		
						Good general health		
						Minimum of twelve months experience		
						Social skills		Date of interview 28/3/98
						Organisation skills		
						Time management		
						Team member		
						Ability to work on own initiative (self-reliant)		
						Leadership qualities		
						Ability to handle stress		
						Numeracy		
						Literacy		
						Flexibility		
						Ability to retail		
						C+G NVQ LEVEL III/C+G Advanced	Desirable attributes	
						Experience in computer reception package		
						Comments		KEY

KEY
✓ if applicant has an essential attribute
✗ if applicant has a desirable attribute

Fig. 3.15(a)   *Example of an interview short listing form for a stylist*

56

							Job title – Beauty therapist	Date of interview 25/1/98
						Interviewee's name		

						CIBTAC Beautician + body therapy/C+G 304/NVQ II + III	Essential attributes	
						CIBTAC Electrical epilation/C+G 305/NVQ LEVEL III		
						Good level of personal presentation		
						Clear voice		
						Pleasant manner		
						Good general health		
						Minimum of twelve months experience		
						Social skills		
						Organisation skills		
						Time management		
						Team member		
						Ability to work on own initiative (self-reliant)		
						Leadership qualities		
						Ability to handle stress		
						Numeracy		
						Literacy		
						Flexibility		
						Ability to retail		
						Aromatherapy training		
						Aromatherapy experience	Desirable attributes	
						Australian Bodycare product knowledge		
						Sothys product and treatment knowledge		
						Sothys product and treatment experience		
						Experience in computer reception package		
						Comments		

KEY

✓ if applicant has an essential attribute

✗ if applicant has a desirable attribute

Fig. 3.15(b)   *Example of an interview short listing form for a beauty therapist*

GOOD PRACTICE ▷

- *Analyse the qualities and attributes of the person required for the job, considering their achievements, special aptitudes, appearance, disposition, interests and circumstances, and identify the essential and desirable qualities and attributes needed to perform the role and responsibilities.*
- *It is important to take up short listed applicants references.*

POINT TO NOTE ▷

If the business is recruiting a replacement member of staff, care must be taken not to simply copy the previous job and person specification. Time must be taken to review the current market and needs of the business.

Interviews

Having short listed the most suitable applicants for the position the manager needs to set the date for interviews and structure the day including times, tasks and staff to be involved. A standard letter notifying the individuals of the details of the day should be drafted and forwarded to them.

The majority of interviews in the hair and beauty sectors will include some kind of trade test and possibly a simple skills test; if the position includes training then it is likely that a training task will be set. It is important for the interviewee to know exactly what they have to do and what they have to bring with them. A trade test will generally involve performing one or more treatments whereas a simple skill test may be simply to ask the applicant to add up the days takings or calculate the commission for a member of staff.

Identifying the right person for the job requires human judgement so it is important that the manager has methodically short listed the applicants and uses a fresh short list form on the day of the interviews to reassess each individual's qualities and attributes.

The interview process is used to analyse the person and to consider their eligibility and suitability for the position.

Eligibility
Qualifications
Experience
References
Performance at interview

Suitability (future performance)
Fitting in with the team
Ability
Versatility
Flexibility
Self assessment by applicant on their suitability

Interviewing – key points
- Structure the process.
- Establish a rapport.

- Control the structure.
- It is important to have prepared well for the day; planning and timing are crucial. It is also essential to build a rapport with the candidates to make them relax and talk openly. The interviewer must remain in control of the interview extracting the information required to build a picture of the applicant and keeping within the time constraints.

POINT TO NOTE ▷ *Some employers use a points system when recruiting staff, awarding points based on qualifications, experience and skills required for the position*

GOOD PRACTICE ▷
- *Always request copies of applicants' professional qualifications and membership of professional organisations.*
- *When using trade tests as part of the interview procedure ensure that the client is someone who will give honest feedback on the applicant's personal/interpersonal skills.*
- *Always ensure that the applicant is eligible (possesses the right qualifications and experience) and suitable (fits in with the team and the management) for the position.*
- *At interview try to gain more than one person's views on the applicant's suitability.*

POINT TO NOTE ▷ *No matter how well qualified and how much experience a new member of staff has the appointment seldom works out if they don't get on with the other staff.*

Interview questions
There are a variety of different types of questions that an interviewer can use, i.e. open, closed, probing, linking, and some that they should avoid, i.e. ambiguous, leading and multiple.

Open questions are used so that the applicant has to provide information, e.g. 'What responsibilities does your present job involve?' Closed questions on the other hand will result in restricted replies of yes or no, e.g. 'You've worked there for six months?' Probing questions are used to investigate further, e.g. 'Tell me why you enjoyed that'. Linking questions are useful for developing and linking the conversation, e.g. 'So after leaving there you – moved there – then what did you do?'

Leading questions usually contain the required reply so should be avoided, e.g. 'Are your reception skills good?' Ambiguous questions are unclear and can be misunderstood, e.g. 'Do you feel happy using the telephone?' as this could be interpreted in a number of ways, i.e. 'Do you answer in a polite manner?' or 'Do you spend all day on the phone?'

Multiple questions do not give the applicant a chance to answer one question before moving on to the next, e.g. 'Do you want to go into hair dressing or beauty therapy, or do you want to specialise in one particular area?'

It is useful for the interviewers to make a list of the questions that they feel will extract the information that they need to judge the eligibility and suitability of the applicant.

At the end of the interview it is important to establish whether the candidate is still interested in the position. If they are and the interviewers feel that they are a strong applicant they must re-establish vital details such as when they can start, acceptable salary (for both parties) and where they can be contacted.

All candidates should be thanked for attending and informed when they will be notified of the outcome of the interview. This is important to all candidates and is common courtesy and will obviously reflect upon the reputation of the business.

Having interviewed all the applicants the interviewers should write up any notes they have made, reflect on all applicants and consider which is the most suitable person for the position. It is important to remember that the weighting on interview should be on the applicant's future performance and not just on past record as they are (in the case of external applicants) moving into a new environment with a new team.

It must be remembered that interviewing is possibly one of the more difficult tasks undertaken by the manager as it is mainly based on human judgment. External candidates may perform wonderfully on the day but turn out not to be suitable whereas internal candidates may not perform as well due to nerves and knowing that the interviewer already knows all about them. Interviewing is certainly a skill that some people possess and others develop from experience.

POINT TO NOTE ▷   *Some of the larger employers may take up a medical reference or examination either to ensure that the applicant is fit for the job or if the job package includes pensions and private medical care.*

ACTIVITY   Within a small group role play interview situations for:

(a) a receptionist in a busy city centre hairdressing and beauty salon

(b) a beauty therapist in a small suburban health clinic

(c) an apprentice hairdresser in a large city centre hairdressing and beauty salon.

GOOD PRACTICE ▷

- *To ensure truthful information is used references should mainly be seen as a mechanism to corroborate factual details such as the position, responsibilities, date of joining and leaving, salary and record of absenteeism.*

- *If the manager knows a referee personally and is happy that they will give an honest description of the applicant then it may be useful to speak with them.*

ACTIVITY

1 Research the roles and responsibilities for the following positions:

(a) full time aromatherapist in a small suburban clinic

(b) part time acupuncturist in a new health clinic

(c) room to let for a McTimoney chiropractor in a well established health clinic

(d) full time experienced beauty therapist for a large health spa

(e) full time nail technician for a large city centre nail clinic

(f) part time receptionist for a busy suburban hair and beauty salon

(g) full time experienced stylist for a cruise ship

(h) full time technician for a hairdressing product company

(i) full time sales representative for a cosmetic company.

2 Draw up a suitable advertisement for each of the above positions and research the most cost-effective place to advertise these.

3 Draft suitable job descriptions and short listing forms for the above positions.

4 Make a list of ten essential questions to ask the candidates at interview for each of the above positions.

Contract of employment

Once the decision has been made as to which applicant is to be offered the post the manager must notify all applicants of the outcome of the interviews and inform the rest of the team. The manager will then need to draw up a written statement of the employee's terms and conditions of employment including their salary or wages, hours of work, notice entitlements and obligations, holiday entitlement, commencement date of employment, job description and workplace location.

By law as soon as an employee commences employment a contract of employment exists as the employer has offered (whether verbally or written) a position, salary, terms and conditions etc. and the employee has accepted. Under the Employment Rights Act 1996 any employee is entitled to a written statement by their employer within two months of the date they commenced employment providing that their employment lasts for one month or more. However, if employment commenced before 30 November 1993 the employee must make a request for a written statement before they become entitled to it.

Ms Simone Horton began employment as a hairstylist with Mrs Delvis Bona proprietor of Hairworks, 23 High Street, Sheffield on 1st June 1997.

Duties

As a hairstylist you will be expected to perform all services (cutting, colouring, perming, relaxing, setting and blow drying) on all female and male clients of all ages and assist in maintaining the tidiness of the salon.

Place of work

Your main place of work will be at the Sheffield salon. However, from time to time you may be asked to undertake demonstrations to the public at various venues around Sheffield to promote the business.

Salary

Your basic pay will be £145.00 per week plus 5% commission of all retail sales and 10% commission after £145 per week on all services. Your pay will be transferred directly to your bank on the 1st day of the month (commencing 1st July 1997). Travel expenses at a rate of 33p per mile will be paid whenever you incur expenditure on behalf of the salon, i.e. demonstrations at venues other than the salon.

Hours/Holiday/Sick leave/pay/Pension

Your working hours will be:

Tuesday–Thursday	9.00 – 5.30
Friday	11.00 – 8.30
Saturday	9.00 – 4.00

You are entitled to 14 days holiday per year plus the statutory public holidays. Sick leave and pay is subject to statutory sick pay. There is no company pension scheme.

Notice

The amount of notice of termination of your employment you are entitled to receive is one month and you are also required to give us one month's notice. Your employment is permanent subject to your general rights of termination under the law.

Disciplinary/Grievance procedure

You are asked to note the company's disciplinary procedure enclosed with this statement.

DISCIPLINARY PROCEDURE

1. A breach of the following rules may result in instant dismissal without warning upon the decision of any two of the salon Directors:-

1.1 Improper acquisition, use of or disclosure of information concerning the business or its clients which may come into your knowledge by reason of employment.

1.2 Any conduct which in the opinion of the salon Directors may have the effect of bringing the integrity and reputation of the salon into disrepute.

2. In the event of the salon Manager being dissatisfied with your work, conduct, time keeping or any other aspect of your employment you may be given a verbal warning as to the matter causing dissatisfaction by a Director of the salon or his/her representative. If after a reasonable period the salon Manager remains dissatisfied with the matter complained of, the matter may be referred to the salon Directors and you may be given a written warning. If the salon Manager continues to be dissatisfied with the matter complained of, the matter will again be referred to the salon Directors and you may be given the statutory minimum notice of dismissal to which you are entiled by virtue of the length of your employment with the salon.

3. If during the course of your employment you receive more than one verbal warning under Clause 2 for any one or number of matters, then you may be given a final written warning that if any matter subsequently warrants further verbal warning you may be dismissed.

4. No disciplinary action will be taken until your case has been investigated by the salon Director. If there is any disciplinary decision relating to you, or you have any grievance relating to your employment, you may apply in writing within fourteen days of such decision or the occasion of such grievance to the salon Directors and you may be accompanied by any one employee of your choice from the salon.

Fig. 3.16   *Example of a written statement of employment*

This written statement does not have to cover every aspect of the contract of employment so it is important for all employers to draw up as much information appertaining to the employee's contract to ensure that if this is to be given verbally they do not miss out any information. A written contract gives both the employee and the employer a certain degree of protection and security and formalises specific points.

A contract of employment generally covers the following points:

- name of the company and the employee
- date when employment began
- job description
- hours of work
- pay scale, how payment will be made and at what intervals (weekly, monthly etc.)
- holiday entitlement
- pension arrangements
- sick leave and sick pay conditions
- length of notice which an employee is entitled to give and receive
- disciplinary procedures
- grievance procedures
- details of probation period
- radius clause; i.e. a clause preventing the employee from taking up another job within a certain specified distance form the salon – this may be added to act mainly as a deterrent as legally it is difficult to enforce.

There are other conditions which may be added such as working at different locations, confidentiality, medical examinations etc. and these are sometimes presented in a separate staff handbook.

Induction

This is a very important stage in an employee's employment and one that is often overlooked within smaller businesses. In order to gain the maximum from the employee it is essential that they fully understand the operations of the business. It would be crazy to employ a receptionist and not give them guidance on the staff, treatments and retail products sold and expect them to make suitable bookings.

Large companies tend to hold formal induction programmes to familiarise the employee with everything about the company. They also tend to have induction handbooks which are sometimes referred to as the company handbook and will include written guidance on the induction programme, clearly identify rules and regulations of the company and explain contractual agreements etc.

An induction may be anything from half a day to three days or even more but it should be designed to:

- familiarise the employee with the business and the standards required of them
- make them feel comfortable with their job and their role within the business
- motivate them
- provide appropriate training, e.g. product, equipment, reception, new skills.

EXAMPLE OF A CONTRACT OF EMPLOYMENT

THIS AGREEMENT dated _____
is made **BETWEEN**

(1) _____ *Salon's name* _____ "The Business"

(2) _____ *Employee's name* _____ "The Employee"

1 Definitions

"Business" the business carried on from time to time by The Business name

"Confidential Information" any trade secrets or any other confidential Information relating to the Business (including information relating to any of the Business customers or anyone else the Business deals with)

"Employment" The Employee's permanent employment under this Agreement

"Incapacity" any illness or similar reason preventing the employee from properly carrying out the employment

"Proprietor" the Proprietor of the Business or from time to time the person having control over the Business. The proprietor at the date of this contract is

_____

2 Job title and length of employment

2.1 The Employee agrees to waive any rights to a redundancy payment and any claim in respect of unfair dismissal under the Employment Protection (Consolidation) Act 1978

2.2 The Business agrees to employ the Employee as a Beauty Therapist from: date _____

2.3 The employment may be brought to an end;

2.3.1 by either party giving the other weeks written notice; or

2.3.2 by the business under Clause 15

2.4 No employment with a previous employer counts as part of the Employee's continuous employment with the Business.

3 Duties

The Employee must:–

3.1 do all in her power to promote, develop and extend the Business

3.2 comply with the directions of the Proprietor

3.3 work in any place which the Proprietor may (reasonably) require.

4 To devote full time

4.1 The Employee must (unless prevented by incapacity) devote his/her whole time and attention to the Business

4.2 The Employee must not without the prior consent of the Proprietor take part in or have an interest in any other business which is simiar or competes with the Business.

5 Pay

The Business agrees to pay the Employee a fixed salary accruing from day to day at the basic rate of £____ per year payable in arrears by equal monthly (weekly, quarterly) installments on the _____ day of each month (week, quarter).

6 Commission

6.1 On the sale of individual courses of treatment to clients commission will be paid to the Employee. The total value of treatments will be calculated on sales within the specified period and commission will be paid at the following rates:–
(a)   Rates of commission to be inserted here

6.2 The Employee will be paid commission on sales of any product sold directly by the employee that is supplied by the Business

6.3 Commission will be based on the sale price of the product less VAT and paid at the following rates:–
(a)   Rate of commission to be inserted here

6.4 Commission will be calculated on sales directly attributable to the Employee in a specified monthly (weekly, quarter) period and the commission will be paid on the day basic salary is paid.

Continued

Fig. 3.17 *Example of a contract of employment*

7 Training courses

Employees will be given regular training courses to update skills and product knowledge.

7.1 If any employee terminates her employment with the Business within a period of One month of completion of a training course, the Employee will be required to refund to the Business 100% (one hundred per cent) of training costs and expenses incurred by the Business.

7.2 If an Employee terminates his/her employment within three months of completing a training course, the Employee will be required to repay the Business 50% (fifty per cent) of training costs/expenses incurred by the Business.

7.3 If an Employee terminates his/her employment within Six months of completion of a training course, the Employee will be required to contribute 25% (twenty-five per cent) of the training costs and expenses incurred by the Business.

7.4 If the Proprietor terminates the Employee's employment, the Employee will not be required to refund any training costs and expenses.

8 Expenses

8.1 The Business agrees to pay the Employee all reasonable expenses wholly and exclusively incurred by him/her in the performance of the employment

8.2 The Employee must give receipts or other evidence of these expenses.

9 Holidays

9.1 The Business holiday year runs from _____ to _____

9.2 The Employee is entitled to_____ working days holiday in each holiday year (in addition to the usual public holidays) to be taken when convenient to the Business

9.3 The Employee must not without consent of the Proprietor carry forward any unused part of his/her holiday to a subsequent holiday year

9.4 The Employee may be required to work on some Bank Holidays and the Employee will be given seven days notice of the requirement to work on a Public/Bank holiday and will be given a proportionate amount of time off in lieu.

10 Hours of employment

Details of hours to worked each week to be stated clearly at this point in the contract

The Employee will be required to work for absenteeism of colleagues at the request of the Proprietor and the Employee covering for absent colleagues will be given a proportionate amount of leave to that extra work undertaken by the Employee to cover for absent colleagues. Alternately, the Employee working additional hours to cover for absent colleagues at the request of the Proprietor may be paid for such additional hours at a rate agreed prior to undertaking the said work agreed with the Proprietor.

11 Pension

The Business has no Pension Scheme which supplies to the Employee or include details of Company Pension Scheme if applicable.

12 Confidentiality during the employment

12.1 The Employee is aware that in the course of the employment he/she may be given or come across confidential information

12.2 The Employee must not disclose or use any confidential information (Except in the proper course of his/her duties)

12.3 The Employee must use his/her best endeavours to prevent any disclosure of any confidential information

12.4 All notes of any confidential information which the Employee acquires or makes during the employment are the property of the Business. When the employment ends (or at any time during the employment, should the Proprietor so request) the employee must hand over these notes to someone duly authorised by the Proprietor to receive them.

13 Confidentiality after the employment ends

After the employment ends the Employee must not disclose or use any Business trade secrets or any other information which is of a sufficiently high degree of confidentially as amounts to a trade secret.

continued overleaf

Fig. 3.17 *Example of a contract of employment (continued)*

14 Unfair competition after the employment ends

14.1 The Business is entitled to protect its confidential information, its goodwill and its trade connection from any unfair competition by the Employee. Therefore:

14.1.1 For six months after the employment ends the Employee agrees not to:

   (a) seek business from any person, firm or company who at any time during the six months immediately preceding the ending of the employment has been a customer of the Business and with whom the Employee has had personal contact or:

   (b) attempt to persuade away from the Business any person who has at any time during the twelve months immediately preceding the ending of the employment been employed by the Business.

Insert salon address

_____

_____

_____

   (c) work within three miles of any other premises of the Business where the Employee was employed for at least Six months in the last eighteen months of Employment.

15 Incapacity

15.1 If the Employee cannot work because of incapacity he/she must immediately tell the Proprietor. The Employee must provide a medical certificate specifying the nature of the incapacity and its likely duration after four days of the start of his/her absence and then at weekly intervals.

15.2 The Employee will be paid during absence due to incapacity Statutory Sick Pay.

16 Grievance procedure

If the Employee has any questions or grievance relating to the employment:

16.1 In the first instance he/she should discuss the matter informally with his/her immediate superior

16.2 If the matter is still unresolved or if the Employee still thinks that he/she has not been fairly treated, he/she may appeal in writing within seven days of the informal discussion.

17 Disciplinary procedure

A copy of the current edition of the Disciplinary Procedure affecting the Employee is available for inspection from the Proprietor at any time.

18 Ending the employment

The Business may end the employment without notice or pay in lieu of the notice on the following circumstances:

18.1 If the Employee has committed a serious or repeated breach of any of his/her obligations under this Agreement (or the Business has reasonable grounds for believing he/she has done so) or:

18.2 If the Employee:–

18.2.1 becomes bankrupt: or:

18.2.2 enters into a voluntary arrangement under the Insolvency Act 1986; or

18.2.3 becomes of unsound mind or becomes a patient under the Mental Health Act 1983: or:

18.2.4 If the Employee has been absent for a period of twenty six weeks (whether consecutive or in aggregated) in any period of two years as a result of incapacity.

19 Effect of ending the employment

19.1 The Employee must still comply with his/her obligations under clauses 12, 13 and 14 of the Agreement even if the Business has committed a breach of this Agreement, however serious

19.2 The ending of the Employment will not affect any rights the Business has against the Employee (or the Employee has against the Business) arising from any breach of this Agreement which occurred before the employment ended.

Signed _____

Dated _____ day of _____ 19 _____

Fig. 3.17 _Example of a contract of employment (continued)_

The induction should include information such as:

- information on the business (e.g. type of, organisational structure, communication mechanisms, appointment and recording systems etc.)
- opportunities for training and promotion
- health and safety procedures (e.g. First Aid facilities, fire regulations, care of, storage, handling and disposal of products and equipment etc.)
- disciplinary and grievance procedures
- salary mechanisms
- sickness and cover procedures
- personal use of business property, e.g. telephone
- introduction to and integration with the team

Larger businesses may provide other information such as:

- pension details
- medical facilities
- catering facilities
- travelling and or subsistence arrangements
- social and welfare arrangements.

Appraisal

Appraisal is the term given to a review of an employee's performance over a given period of time, normally annually. The main reason for operating an appraisal system is to help the employee become more effective. The actual mechanisms used for appraisal will vary from employer to employer and are often dependent upon the size of the business. A large employer is likely to have a very structured more formal approach to appraisal whereas a smaller employer will tend to use more informal mechanisms. Whatever system the employer uses the aim will be the same – to maximise staff potential to increase productivity. Therefore, appraisal is a very important managerial role that must not be forgotten even in a small business.

The appraisal is normally categorised into the following areas:

- Review
- Looking back over the period concerned, what is the appraisee's job, and has it altered in any way? Is it being performed effectively? Are there any problems?
- Action
- What needs to be done? Should there be any training and development? Does the employee need more support/guidance?
- Monitoring
- Are the actions being carried out? Are targets being achieved?

Reasons for appraisal

The reasons for appraisal are that it:

- provides employees with feedback on their individual performance
- provides a basis for promotion, dismissal, probation etc.

- provides staff with a basis for self evaluation
- provides a mechanism for reviewing salary, commission rates, conditions of service etc.
- provides a mechanism for identifying staff potential, development and training
- provides a mechanism for monitoring the effectiveness of policies and procedures.

It is fairly common practice within larger business for a self-appraisal form to be issued to employees prior to the appraisal interview. This affords them the opportunity to provide information on how they perceive their performance in their job, position, roles and responsibilities.

Appraisal interview – manager's checklist

1 Prior to the interview consider the type of questions to be used, e.g. open to gain information, closed to check or confirm information etc.
2 Decide what information is required and make a list of the main points.
3 If applicable issue a self-appraisal form.
4 Set a date and time for the interview
5 At the interview explain clearly to the employee the purpose of the interview, make them feel comfortable and agree an agenda that is acceptable to both the employee and the employer.
6 Ensure that the employee realises the appraisal is a two-way discussion and feels able to talk freely.
7 Ensure that any points raised by the employee are addressed.
8 Throughout the interview focus on the employee's responsibilities rather than their character traits (unless there is a particular problem) and make notes on the agreed action etc. as it is impossible to remember everything.
9 Handle any apathy and disagreements constructively and focus on how they can be resolved.
10 Remember to listen carefully to what is being said or left out!
11 After the interview ensure that the agreements formed in it are acted upon.

GOOD PRACTICE ▷   *In larger businesses where appraisal is often carried out by a number of people, often across different teams or buildings, evaluation forms based on the actual appraisal mechanisms are used to provide feedback to the company on the appraisal system.*

POINT TO NOTE ▷   *Ultimately appraisal should be a positive system allowing both the employee and the manager to develop a better understanding of one another. It should lead to increased motivation and provide a basis for reward where this may otherwise be difficult, as in the case of commission etc.*

Name of appraisee ....
Job title ....
Date of appraisal ....
Name of inline manager/supervisor ....

1. Please identify any duties that are undertaken by the appraisee that are not identified in their job description.
   ....
   ....

2. Pleae list the areas of work in which the appraisee has been most successful.
   ....
   ....

3. Please list the areas of work in which the appraisee has been least successful.
   ....
   ....

4. Please list any factors that have had an effect on the appraisee's performance over the past year.
   ....
   ....

5. How will the appraisee's role develop over:
   (a) the next twelve months ....
   ....
   ....

   (b) the next two–three years. ....
   ....

6. Please list what additional support the appraisee will need in terms of training development in the following areas:
   (a) skills ....
   ....

   (b) knowledge ....
   ....

   (c) sales ....
   ....

   (d) social/life skills ....
   ....

   (e) team building/leadership ....
   ....

   (f) Other areas not covered by (a)–(e) above. ....
   ....

7. What are the agreed targets and time scales for the appraisee development?
   ....

8. Inline manager/supervisor's comments
   ....

9. Appraisee's comments
   ....

10. Date of next appraisal ....

Signature .... (Inline manager/supervisor)   Date ....

Singature .... (Appraisee)   Date ....

Fig. 3.18 *Example of an appraisal form*

ACTIVITY

1   Devise self-appraisal forms suitable for the following:

(a) a small hairdressing salon employing a stylist and a junior

(b) a city centre hair and beauty salon employing a manager, three stylists, a modern apprentice, a receptionist and two beauty therapists

(c) a natural health clinic with a reflexologist who is the owner and employs two aromatherapists and hires out two rooms throughout the week to a chiropractor, an iridologist, an acupuncturist and a reiki practitioner.

2   Make a list of the types of questions you could use during an appraisal interview for:

(a) a modern hairdressing apprentice

(b) an experienced stylist/supervisor

(c) an experienced beauty therapist

(d) an experienced holistic practitioner.

Staff development

The success of the business lies in expansion and not remaining static; new treatments and ideas should be periodically introduced to increase profit margins, attract new clients and to keep abreast of changes.

Staff should be regularly sent on training courses whether they be for product knowledge, new technical skills, developing their personal and interpersonal skills or for obtaining further qualifications. Well-structured staff development will help to ensure a highly motivated work force boosting staff morale.

Many employers are fully aware of the benefits of offering retail products to their staff at cost price, of ensuring that they have experienced all of the salon treatments on offer to the clients, as well as ensuring that the staff have treatments to benefit their individual needs. The image of the salon is reflected by the appearance of the staff. When was the last time you saw a sales assistant in a top fashion retail outlet dressed in scruffy out-of-date clothes?

POINTS TO NOTE ▷

● *It is useful for the practitioner to have treatments in the salon and to role play the treatment as a realistic client, noting the way the reception area looked and how the receptionist and therapist interacted with them and each other.*

● *Staff development may be required to improve technical skills, e.g. new treatments, techniques or product knowledge, or for personal behavioural development such as team building.*

KEY TERMS

You need to know what these words and phrases mean. Go back through the chapter to find out.

Organisational structure
Employer
Manager
Personal and interpersonal skills/
  key skills
Communication
Listening skills
Personal presentation
Social skills
Time management

Numeracy/literacy skills
IT
The receptionist
Recruitment
Interview selection
Contract of employment
Induction
Appraisal
Staff development

4 Business legislation

This chapter covers the following areas:
➤ employment legislation
➤ treatment and consumer legislation.

Fig. 4.1 *Spa at sea*

This chapter explains existing business legislation but it must be stressed that it is the employer's responsibility to keep abreast of changing legislation and regulations regarding employment, treatments and consumer safety.

Employment legislation

Today the majority of workers in the UK are relatively well protected by government legislation but in the past this was not always the case. Prior to the nineteenth century the health and safety of the workforce was not a concern of employers, then with the growth of trade unions and assistance from some individuals conditions in the workplace gradually changed and pressure on a number of governments brought about legislation to improve working conditions.

Businesses employing more than five employees will, as a result of the Health and Safety at Work Act (1974), issue a written health and safety policy which is generally presented and explained to employees at their induction. A health and safety policy clearly outlines to employees the company's aims and objectives on health and safety. It is important to note that all companies must adhere to current legislation when setting down such a document. This policy can also be used in smaller businesses to assist employees in understanding the employer's commitment to health and safety.

Health and Safety at Work Act (HASAWA) (1974)

This piece of legislation gives rights to both employers and employees.

Employers must provide:

- a safe and healthy workplace including maintenance of a reasonable working temperature of not less than 16 °C after the first opening hour, effective ventilation, suitable lighting and humidity levels and adequate toilets and washing facilities
- proper safety procedures – fire exits, notices, drills, handling and recording of accidents etc.
- safe equipment which is regularly serviced
- adequate training for all staff in safety procedures
- access to a written local health and safety policy.

Employees must:

- follow health and safety procedures
- act to protect themselves and others
- treat all equipment properly and report any faults.

POINT TO NOTE ▷ **Accidents within the workplace**

Unfortunately despite legislation and employers' efforts to prevent accidents within the workplace they do happen whether through human error or environmental causes. It is therefore important for procedures in the case of accidents to be included as part of staff induction. This should include information on handling possible accidents, names of first aiders, location of first aid box and procedure for recording such occurrences in the business accident book.

Electricity at Work Regulations Act (1990)

This piece of legislation states that all pieces of electrical equipment in the workplace should be checked annually by a qualified electrician. In particular, discontinue using any equipment that is broken or damaged, displays exposed wires or worn flexes or has a cracked or broken plug.

Also, you should take care never to overload sockets. Within a health and beauty and hairdressing business there is likely to be a great deal of portable equipment, e.g. hair dryers, epilation units etc. which it is essential to have tested annually.

GOOD PRACTICE ▷ *Many establishments take out a contract with either the equipment providers or a local company to undertake maintenance and testing of electrical equipment. If in doubt, contact your local trade wholesaler for recommendations of suitable people.*

Fire Precautions Act (1971)

This piece of legislation states that all employees should be trained and aware of emergency fire evacuation procedures. This should include such things as:

- the nearest fire exit (this should remain unlocked with clear access during working hours)
- the appropriate assembly point that everyone should meet at once the building has been evacuated
- in the event of a fire lifts must not be used
- where possible all windows and doors should be closed on leaving the premises
- all personal belongings should be left behind when evacuating the premises
- an awareness of the location and type of fire fighting equipment available on the premises.

Extinguisher	Type of fire
Blue (dry powder)	Multi-purpose
Red (water)	Solid material
Black (carbon dioxide (CO_2) gas)	Electrical
Green (halon gas)	Electrical
Cream (foam)	Liquids
Red (blanket)	Liquids and cloth

Fig. 4.2 *Fire-fighting equipment checklist*

GOOD PRACTICE ▷ *Each business should hold regular fire drills to ensure that their employees are fully prepared for their own safety and that of the clients in the event of a fire.*

The Control of Substances Hazardous to Health Regulations (COSHH) (1988)

These regulations lay down the ways in which substances which can be deemed hazardous to health (e.g. hydrogen peroxide) should be used and stored. Employers are responsible for assessing risks from hazardous substances and deciding upon action to reduce them. The majority of manufacturers issue clear instructions on the handling of products that fall within these regulations. It is essential that all employees should be made aware of the risks of such substances and where necessary be given training in such areas. Employees should always follow safety guidelines and take the precautions identified by their employer.

GOOD PRACTICE ▷

In case a client becomes ill whilst waiting for or having treatment, it would be useful if the practitioner noted an emergency contact number on each of their clients' record cards.

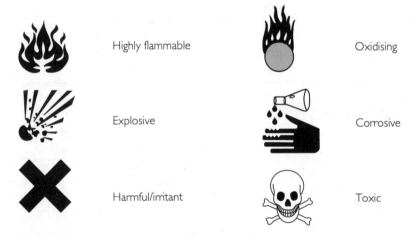

Fig. 4.3 *Common symbols used for substances hazardous to health*

Examples of hazardous substances that may be found within a health, beauty or hairdressing environment

Highly flammable

Highly flammable substances, e.g. acetone and solvents are deemed hazardous to health because if their vapours are exposed to naked flames or other means of extreme heat they can ignite.

Recommended storage

These products must be kept sealed and stored in a cool place. It is important not to store large quantities together as in the event of a fire they would cause a large explosion.

You should also be aware that some products are more flammable than others, e.g. ethanol-based products such as witch-hazel are far less flammable than acetone-based products such as nail varnish remover.

Recommended handling and usage

It is important to use flammable products in an area that is well ventilated and not to dispense them in an area where there is a risk of fire, e.g whilst someone is smoking, near a naked flame or near an area of extreme heat. Extreme care must be taken when transferring products into dispensing containers to ensure that the labels are clear and correct. Care must be taken when using the product to avoid excessive inhalation, or contact with eyes and skin.

In the event that the product comes into contact with the eyes or skin emergency first aid of rinsing with water should be given immediately. If the casualty continues to have any sign of irritation they must be referred for medical advice. Medical advice must be sought if the product has been in contact with the eye or ingested. In the case of inhalation the person must be moved into fresh air.

Recommended disposal

These types of products must not be disposed of via sanitary systems as this leads to pollution. Advice on disposal should be sought from the practitioner's local environmental health and trading standards department.

Recommended action

In the event of a fire evacuate the premises and notify the fire brigade of the location of stored flammables.

POINTS TO NOTE ▷

- *Acetone is used as a solvent in nail enamel removers. It can cause splitting and peeling of the nails and skin rashes on the fingers and hands. Inhalation of acetone can irritate the lungs.*
- *Alkyl sodium sulphates are used in shampoos for their cleaning ability and ease of rinsing from the hair. They may cause irritation to the skin.*
- *Ethanol is a colourless, clear and very flammable cosmetic ingredient. It is used as an antibacterial agent in mouth washes, liquid lip rouge, nail enamel, astringents etc. It is also used medicinally as a topical antiseptic, blood vessel dilator and sedative.*
- *Ethanolamide of lauric acid is used in soapless shampoos and is a mild skin irritant.*
- *Ether is used as a solvent in nail polishes. It is a mild skin irritant.*
- *Ethoxyethanol is used as a solvent and plasticiser for nail enamels. It is toxic when applied direct to the skin.*
- *Hydrogen peroxide is an ingredient used in skin bleaches, hair bleaches, permanent colours and cold permanent waves for it's oxidising and bleaching ability. If used undiluted it can cause burns to the skin.*
- *Salicylic acid is obtained from sweet birch, wintergreen leaves and other plants. It is used in small percentages as an antimicrobial and preservative in cosmetics such as face masks, hair tonics, hair dye removers, deodorants, suntan lotions etc. In medicines it is used in higher quantities in ointments, plasters, powders and lotions. Absorption via the skin may cause irritation such as skin rashes, vomiting, increased respiration and abdominal pain.*

ACTIVITY

Select ten cosmetics from a bathroom, list their ingredients and research the effect of each.

List the products that due to their ingredients should be stored out of direct sunlight.

Explosive
Aerosols, e.g. hairspray, nail dry sprays, deodorants and air fresheners, are deemed hazardous to health as they are flammable and are explosive under certain heat-induced conditions.

Recommended storage
These products must be stored in a dry, cool place and away from direct sunlight.

Recommended handling and usage
Any product considered to be flammable should only be used within an area that is well ventilated. Care must be taken when handling such products to avoid contact with the eyes.

It is important when using aerosol/spay containers not to heat the canister or to tamper with the actuator. Care must be taken when using the product to avoid excessive inhalation and not to dispense it on to or near a naked flame or a very hot surface, which might cause combustion and fire.

Recommended disposal
In the event of a spillage, ventilate the area then, wearing disposable gloves and using a cloth or tissue, wipe up the spillage immediately.

Unless stated by the manufacture dispose of small quantities in the normal manner ensuring that the canister can not be pierced or placed in extreme heat.

Recommended action
In the event of a fire evacuate the premises and notify the fire brigade of the location of stored aerosols.

POINTS TO NOTE ▷

- *Aerosol products under pressure when exposed to excessive heat e.g. in direct strong sunlight can explode and burst into flames*
- *Ensure canisters are not pierced and do not burn them.*

Harmful/irritant products
Products such as hydrogen peroxide are deemed hazardous to health as they may cause irritation whether through direct contact, inhalation or absorption.

Recommended storage

These products should be stored carefully in a cool place within the business premises to avoid unnecessary exposure and possible irritation. The products must retain their lids and labels.

Recommended handling and usage

Care must be taken when handling harmful products including the wearing of gloves to protect the hands. Spillages must be removed immediately.

Recommended disposal

The majority of these products used within the health, beauty and hairdressing environment can be disposed of in the normal manner. It is important to observe manufacturer's instructions and if necessary seek the advice of the environmental health and trading standards department within the local authority.

Recommended action

Observe standard first aid procedures if ingredients come into contact with the eyes or skin or if inhaled or ingested.

POINT TO NOTE ▷ *It is important to remember that current legislation must be observed, in particular the Local Government (miscellaneous provisions) Act of 1982 which advises on the use and disposal of equipment such as needles used by practitioners for treatments such as acupuncture, electrolysis and ear piercing.*

Health and safety legislation – the 'six pack' (1992)

The new health and safety at work legislation is commonly referred to as the 'six pack' and was introduced to fulfil European Union directives. It is composed of:

1 The Management of Health and Safety at Work Regulations (1992)

This is to ensure that the correct systems are in place to co-ordinate, control and monitor health and safety management. This regulation requires the employer to:

- assess the health and safety risks to employees, clients and other visitors to the business premises
- plan, implement, monitor and review preventative measures
- maintain accurate health and safety records, e.g servicing and repair of equipment
- select and appoint appropriate people to implement fire evacuation procedures and first aid
- ensure that all employees are provided with detailed information on the company's health and safety procedures and are adequately trained and updated in these.

78

2 Provision and Use of Work Equipment Regulations (1992)

The aim of this legislation is to clarify and join together the many regulations relating to equipment. This legislation ensures that all equipment, whether new or second hand, must be properly maintained and all employees must be correctly trained in how to use and maintain it. It also ensures that written records regarding its maintenance are accurately kept.

3 Manual Handling Operations Regulations (1992)

This is to ensure that proper procedures are laid down by the employer for the manual handling of goods etc. within the workplace, e.g. lifting heavy loads which often results in industrial injury.

4 Workplace (Health, Safety and Welfare) Regulations (1992)

These are to clarify and link together previous legislation relating to the working environment, safety facilities and 'housekeeping'.

5 Personal Protective Equipment at Work (PPE) Regulations (1992)

These are to clarify and join together previous legislation including the use, type and storage of personal protective equipment. It is the employer's responsibility to ensure that all employees who may be at risk of being exposed to health risks or injury are provided, free of charge, with appropriate protective equipment. They must also ensure that such equipment is maintained in good working order and that all employees are trained in its use.

6 Health and Safety (Display Screen Equipment) Regulations (1992)

These are to clearly identify rules and regulations to protect the health and safety of employees who use display screen equipment. As the use of computers in businesses has rapidly expanded these regulations were needed to ensure employees are protected from eye strain, muscular pain, etc. These regulations apply to both new and second-hand equipment and require employers to assess the work area and equipment to prevent risk of strain or injury to employees and to provide suitable desks, chairs and, if needed, spectacles along with the appropriate training.

POINT TO NOTE ▷   *Inspectors of the Health and Safety Executive (HSE) are at liberty to enter any business at a reasonable time and investigate claims of unsafe practice with regard to health and safety. The inspectors have the power to serve an improvement notice if they find fault under the health and safety regulations. The improvement notice must state the fault and the time limit given to rectify the fault, which is usually twenty one days. If the inspectors finds that the fault may endanger personal safety they will serve a prohibition notice which requires the employer to cease activity immediately or face criminal prosecution.*

Statistics on health and safety are issued from time to time by the HSE.

The Safety Representative and Safety Committees Regulations (1977)

This legislation ensures that safety representatives are appointed from the membership of a trade union recognised by the employer. It is their remit to liaise with the employers on all matters relating to health and safety. The number of representatives will obviously be dependent on a number of points, including the quantity of employees, the variety of occupations housed within the organisational structure and the varying types of work activities undertaken. It is the responsibility of the union to put forward their nominee in writing. This person must have been employed by the organisation for at least two years or have 'similar' employment experience in the previous two years. Once officially appointed to the role of health and safety representative the employee is entitled to time off for relevant training for the role, e.g. to attend seminars and meetings. The employer must give the representative sufficient consultation time on any new issues concerning health and safety.

The Health and Safety (First Aid) Regulations (1981)

These regulations lay down the minimum requirements for the provision of first aid in the workplace. The requirements will obviously vary according to the number of employees and the type of work performed within the business. There should be at least one employee who has received training in first aid and continues to keep their skills current, e.g. a St. John's Ambulance First Aid certificate has to be renewed every three years.

First aid box

A standard first aid kit in the workplace should contain the following:

- guidance card
- sterile dressings of various sizes
- individually wrapped adhesive dressings
- eye pads
- triangular bandages
- safety pins.

The quantity of each of the above items will be dependent on the workplace. The contents should all be kept in a damp and dust-proof container which is exclusively used for first aid purposes. It is important to note that from time to time regulations may change or be updated. The container must be clearly labelled in accordance with current regulations.

GOOD PRACTICE ▷ *Always check the current regulations regarding the contents of a workplace first aid box.*

Problem	Priority	Action
Minor cuts	To stop the bleeding	Apply pressure over cotton wool taking care to avoid contact with the blood.
Severe cuts	To stop the bleeding	Keep applying pressure over a clean towel until qualified help arrives. Put on disposable gloves as soon as possible.
Electric shock	To remove from source of electricity	Do not touch the person until they are disconnected from the electricity supply. If breathing has stopped, artifical respiration will need to be given by a qualified person. Ring for an ambulance.
Dizziness	To restore the flow of blood to the head	Position the person with their head down between their knees and loosen their clothing.
Fainting	To restore the flow of blood to the head	Lie the person down with their feet raised on a cushion.
Nose bleed	To constrict the flow of blood	Sit the client up with their head bent forward. Loosen the clothing around their neck. Pinch the soft part of their nose firmly until bleeding has stopped. Make sure breathing continues through the mouth during this period. If bleeding has not stopped after half an hour, medical attention must be sought.
Burns	To cool the skin and prevent it from breaking	Hold the affected area under cold, running water until the pain is relieved. Serious burns should be covered loosely with a sterile dressing and medical attention sought.
Epilepsy	To prevent self-injury and relieve embarrassment	Do not interfere forcibly with a person during an attack. Gently prevent them from injuring themselves. Ensure the person's airways are clear and wipe away any froth which forms at the mouth. After the attack, cover with a blanket, comfort and give reassurance until recovery is complete.
Objects in the eye	To remove the object without damaging the eye	Expose the invaded area and try stroking the object towards the inside corner of the eye with a dampened twist of cotton wool. If this is not successful, help the person to use an eye bath containing clean warm water.
Falls	To determine if there is spine damage. To treat minor injuries if the fall is not serious	If the person complains of pains in the back or neck, then do not move them: cover them with a warm blanket and get medical aid immediately. For less serious falls, treat the bruises, cuts, sprains or grazes as appropriate.

Fig. 4.4   *First aid situations the practitioner may have to deal with*

POINT TO NOTE ▷   *The first aid requirements of a workplace will vary according to:*
- *the number of employees*
- *the nature of the work undertaken within the business*
- *the size and layout of the business premises*
- *the employer's first aid policy.*

The Reporting of Injuries, Diseases and Dangerous Occurrences Regulations (1985)

These regulations cover all employees and members of the public who as a result of work-based activity suffer a condition or an injury

The Environmental Protection Act (1990)

This Act relates to the safe disposal of hazardous substances. It ensures that any practitioner using hazardous substances must ensure that disposal of them does not cause harm to the environment or individuals.

The Sex Discrimination Acts (1975, 1986) and The Race Relations Act (1976)

The aim of these acts is to prevent direct or indirect discrimination against candidates applying for work on the grounds of race, sex, or marital status. The Equal Opportunities Commission will investigate complaints made on any of the above grounds and it monitors job advertisements as well.

POINT TO NOTE ▷ *An employee can seek unfair dismissal on grounds of sex discrimination through an industrial tribunal irrespective of length of service.*

Equal Pay Act (1970)

The aim of this Act was to ensure that people who undertake the same work must be employed on the same terms and pay.

ACTIVITY

Although there are laws relating to offences for equal opportunities the employer is not obliged by law to be an equal opportunities employer.

(a) Look through the classified section in your trade journal and local newspaper, and make a list of the number of advertisements which state that the employer is an equal opportunities employer.

(b) Classify the type of organisations which state that they are equal opportunities employers.

The Disability Discrimination Act (1995)

This Act covers people who have had a disability in the past as well as those who are currently registered disabled. The disability of a person is defined in the Act as either a physical or mental impairment which has a substantial long-term effect on an individual's ability to carry out what are considered to be normal day-to-day activities. This Act has several clauses and one of these relates to employment making it unlawful for employers who have twenty or more staff to discriminate against any current or prospective employee because of a reason relating to their disability. Responsibilities of employers include such things as making reasonable changes to the working environment and general employment arrangements so that the disabled employee is not disadvantaged compared to their able-bodied colleagues.

There are exemptions under this Act such as:

- police officers
- people serving in the armed services
- fire officers
- prison officers etc.

The Employment Rights Act (1996)

This Act supersedes some of the points in The Trade Union and Employment Rights Act (1993) which was designed to improve the employment rights of part-time workers. It entitled all female employees to take up to fourteen weeks maternity leave irrespective of their length of service with the organisation. It also gave all employees, after a period of time, the right to be given written terms and conditions of employment and it enabled all employees to appeal against unfair dismissal.

The Employment Rights Act of 1996 states that an employee is entitled to ask for a written statement of their terms and conditions of employment after one month's employment, and have the right to receive this after the expiry of two months from the date of commencement of employment. This Act does not refer to a contract of employment but does give an employer a legal obligation to supply a written statement which should contain details of the salary or wages, hours of work, notice entitlements and obligations, holiday entitlement, date of commencement of employment, job description and workplace location. This Act does not require the employer to title the document as a contract, although in employment law the employee is deemed to have a contract of employment when the offer by the employer of the job and the acceptance by the employee indicates an intention to enter into a legally binding relationship.

If the employer does not provide the written statement then the employee has the right to make an application to an industrial tribunal who can order the employer to produce the written statement.

POINT TO NOTE ▷ *An employee who is dismissed whilst pursuing their right to a written statement of their terms and conditions of employment will have unfair dismissal protection irrespective of their length of employment.*

GOOD PRACTICE ▷ *A contract of employment can be used to the employer's advantage if probationary periods and performance targets have been included, agreed upon and are not fulfilled.*

Misrepresentation Act (1967)

This legislation protects a person who enters into a contract and allows them the opportunity to make a claim based on misrepresentation of terms which causes them to suffer damage.

GOOD PRACTICE ▷ *It is essential for the manager to keep abreast of any changes in the employment law. It may be in the case of a small business due to restricted legal knowledge that they decide to take advice from a legal business advisor.*

POINT TO NOTE ▷ *An employee's statutory rights generally include the following:*

- *a detailed pay statement indicating what they have earnt and what deductions the employer has made*
- *for them not to be discriminated against*
- *equal pay for equal work*
- *at least one week's notice of dismissal if they have been employed for two months*
- *statutory sick pay*
- *statutory maternity pay*
- *a healthy and safe working environment*
- *after two years of employment with the same company they have the right to redundancy payment*
- *the right to complain to an industrial tribunal if they feel that they have been unfairly dismissed*
- *the right to retain their employment under the same conditions should the business be taken over by another company*
- *the right to be a member of a trade union.*

These rights are not affected by the signing of a contract of employment, which usually states 'this contract does not affect your statutory rights'.

Statutory sick pay (SSP)

All employees over the age of sixteen years of age are entitled to the payment of statutory sick pay (SSP) after they have been off work through illness for four consecutive days from their employer. The employer by law must pay this minimum amount to the employee and they must maintain records of SSP and the employee sickness for inspection by the Department of Social Security (DSS). These records must include details of the dates of absenteeism due to sickness and the days that the employee would normally be at work, i.e. the qualifying days which are generally Monday-Friday, but in the health, beauty and hairdressing industries are highly likely to be different.

POINTS TO NOTE ▷
- *An employee is not entitled to SSP if they are off work for less than four consecutive days.*
- *An employer is liable to pay SSP for the first twenty-eight weeks of an employee's absence due to sickness. This payment is subject to sufficient income tax and national insurance contributions.*
- *A employer may claim reimbursement of SSP from the DSS.*

Maternity rights

In England and Wales women employees who satisfy the relevant qualifying conditions are entitled to the following statutory rights:

- paid time off to receive antenatal care. A woman who is advised by a properly qualified person to attend an antenatal clinic has the right not to be unreasonably refused time off during her working hours to enable her to keep an appointment.
- maternity pay, which is currently payable for eighteen weeks to a woman absent from work because of her pregnancy. There are certain qualifying requirements, however.
- the right to return to work after confinement. A woman can currently return to work at any time before the end of the period of twenty-nine weeks beginning with the week in which the date of confinement falls.

POINT TO NOTE ▷
A woman is automatically held to be unfairly dismissed if the sole reason or principal reason for the dismissal is either that she is pregnant or any other reason connected with the pregnancy.

Disciplinary procedures

All employees should receive a copy of the company's disciplinary procedure within their contract of employment. This will detail the company's policy for dealing with what it considers to be misconduct. The employee should be given a breakdown of the areas of misconduct. There should also be a description of the disciplinary action taken, i.e. verbal warning, written warning etc., the level of management to be involved in such a scenario together with an appeals procedure.

The majority of employers will stipulate that an employee will be given one verbal warning of misconduct followed by a formal (verbal and written) warning and a final written (verbal and written) warning followed by dismissal. Immediate suspension may take place if gross misconduct occurs, e.g. theft.

GOOD PRACTICE ▷ *The employer should:*
- *always investigate alleged misconduct*
- *involve all parties concerned*
- *allow time for improved conduct before taking further steps*
- *ensure that apart from an extremely serious offence no employee should be dismissed on the first occasion*
- *ensure that dismissal is fair before taking action.*

POINT TO NOTE ▷ *Large companies tend to have their own clearly defined grievance and disciplinary procedures.*

GOOD PRACTICE ▷ *A written disciplinary procedure should:*
- *indicate who it applies to*
- *ensure it allows for swift action*
- *state clearly the stages of disciplinary action*
- *state clearly which managerial staff have responsibility for disciplinary procedures*
- *allow for employees to be notified of any complaints against them*
- *allow for employees to put forward their case*
- *allow the employees to be accompanied by a representative, e.g. from a trade union, or another employee.*
- *allow for full investigation before the disciplinary action is taken*
- *allow the employee the right to appeal.*

ACTIVITY

Design a grievance/disciplinary procedure suitable for a large hair and beauty chain ensuring that the following points are taken into consideration:
- protection of and respect for the physical and human resources of the company
- accurate, truthful completion of records, e.g. bookings, time keeping, stock taking etc.
- employee's attendance, e.g. time keeping, illness etc.
- confidentiality
- rules and regulations relating to food, drink etc.

Termination of employment and redundancy

The manager at some time during their career may have to consider action or even possible termination of an employee's employment. It is paramount that they must consider carefully the legal implications such as unfair dismissal and ensure that they observe fully the employer's and employee's rights. It is wise to contact the local Advisory, Conciliation and Arbitration Service (ACAS) office for current legislation and advice.

Unfair dismissal – The Employment Protection (Consolidation) Act (1978)

Under the Employment Protection Act (1978) an employee may claim unfair dismissal if they can prove that the employer has acted in an unlawful manner. The employee must have worked for the organisation for at least two years.

Grounds for unfair dismissal are:

- the joining of a trade union or choosing not to join a trade union.
- alleged redundancy due to the business changing ownership
- any other area where an employer does not adhere to stipulated procedures.

Unfair dismissal can also be sought, irrespective of the employee's length of service, on the grounds of:

- pregnancy
- discrimination due to the sex, race or marital status of an individual.

All of these rights are not affected by the signing of a contract of employment, which usually states 'this contract does not affect your statutory rights'.

POINT TO NOTE ▷   *If an employee thinks they have been unfairly dismissed they will need to take their case to an industrial tribunal. This legal body will listen to both sides of a case and act accordingly.*

GOOD PRACTICE ▷   *The Advisory, Conciliation and Arbitration Service (ACAS) can be contacted by employers to obtain current information on legal practice. The address is:* ACAS, *Clifton House, 83–117 Euston Road, London NW1 2RB.*

Treatment and consumer legislation

This legislation relates to services offered within the business and its environment.

Local bylaws concerning body massage treatments

In England and Wales licensing is controlled by the local authorities. Anyone wishing to set up a clinic offering body massage treatments may need a license to practise, depending upon the area of the country in which their business is located. This license is obtained from the local authority through the Environmental and Trading Standards Department. To qualify for such a license the applicant normally submits information concerning their premises, staff and qualifications. Inspection of the premises is then carried out and once approved by the authority an annual fee, which varies from authority to authority, is paid.

Local Government (Miscellaneous Provisions) Act (1982)

This Act is monitored through the local Environmental Health and Trading Standards Department (EHTS). Any practitioner using needles for treatments, such as acupuncture, epilation, sclerotherapy, collagen injections, semi-permanent make up or ear piercing, must apply for a license to practice under the above Act. This is to ensure that correct hygienic practices are used for storage, use and disposable of 'sharp' implements.

The Sale and Supply of Goods Act (1994)

This Act replaces the Supply of Goods and Services Act (1982) and the Sale of Goods Act (1979). It relates to all goods including food regardless of where they are purchased. Terms under the Act state that the seller has to ensure that the goods are:

● of satisfactory quality : this is defined as the standard that would be regarded by a reasonable person as satisfactory having taken into account the description of the goods, the price and any other relevant circumstances

● reasonably fit: the goods must be able to meet whatever the seller claims they do, e.g. a car must reach 0–60 miles per hour in the number of minutes stated.

Once the contract has been made between the seller and the buyer this Act can be enforced. Verbal and written contracts are both classed as valid contracts and a buyer is entitled to have either their money back or goods replaced if the contract is broken.

POINT TO NOTE ▷

● *Under the Sale and Supply of Goods Act (1994) a buyer does not have to accept a credit note if the contract between the seller and buyer is broken.*

● *The buyer is not entitled to a refund or exchange of goods if at the time of purchase they were told about the faults but chose to ignore them or if they did not see obvious faults.*

Office of Fair Trading (OFT)

The Office of Fair Trading (OFT) is responsible for the administration of policy competition in the UK. It controls monopolies, mergers and consumer protection, e.g. it investigates consumers' complaints about inaccurate trade descriptions.

Trade Descriptions Act (1968, 1972)

This Act makes it a criminal offence to describe goods falsely, and to sell or offer for sale goods which have been so described. It covers many things including advertisements, display cards, oral descriptions and applies to quality, quantity, fitness for purpose and price. The part of the Act passed in 1972 deals with labelling of the country of origin; a product must be clearly labelled so that the consumer can see where it was made.

The Consumer Credit Act (1974)

This Act ensures that the actual rate of interest charged for credit facilities must be highlighted to a borrower.

The Prices Act (1974)

This ensures that prices should be displayed so as not to give a false impression to potential buyers.

The Resale Prices Act (1964, 1976)

This Act prevents manufactures from enforcing retailers of their products to charge a certain price. However, it does not prevent them from supplying a recommended retail price.

The Consumer Safety Act (1978)

This Act identifies the standards for legal safety to reduce the possible risk to consumers from products that may be potentially dangerous or harmful.

The Consumer Protection Act (1987)

This Act deals with three main subjects: product liability, general safety requirements and misleading prices. It follows European directives to safeguard the consumer from unsafe products.

Environmental Health and Trading Standards Departments (EHTS)

Trading standards officers are employed by local authorities and their remit is to investigate complaints from consumers against businesses. Having investigated the complaint they have the authority to take the business to court to prevent reoccurrence of the complaint.

The British Standards Institution (kite marks and safety standards)

The British Standard Institution (BSI) is an independent body which sets voluntary standards of reliability and quality. Its objectives are to:

- establish quality standards
- promote health and safety
- protect the environment.

Manufacturers submit their products for testing voluntarily for them to be tested on such things as their safety, quality, strength etc. The kite marks of the institution are displayed by many business to provide the consumer with a guarantee that they have recognition from the board, indicating that the product has been tested and approved. Examples of such quality marks include the BSI kite mark, the British Gas Seal of Service and the Investors in People Award (see Fig. 4.5).

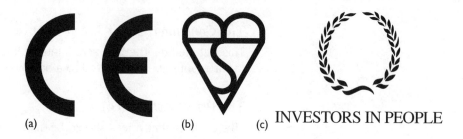

(a)　　　　　　　　(b)　　　(c) INVESTORS IN PEOPLE

Fig. 4.5 *Quality marks (a) European quality specification; (b) BSI kite mark and (c) Investors in People Award*

Data Protection Act (1984)

Practitioners using computers to store personal data on their clients must comply with the Data Protection Act of 1984 which requires them to register with the Data Protection Registrar, or they are liable to face prosecution. The Act only applies to computer information stored relating to living persons. It does not cover manually stored records unless these are made under the Consumer Credit Act.

Information and forms are available from Post Offices and there is a fee for a three-year licence, however small business can complete a simplified registration form. The application requires information on what is stored on the computer, its uses, sources and to whom the data may be disclosed.

Anyone who feels that they are affected by lost or incorrect information or disclosure of personally held computer data without their consent may make a claim to the Registrar. They can be told who holds data on them and for a nominal fee (maximum of £10) are entitled to see these records within 40 days of payment. NB When completing client records careful consideration should be given to the terminology used.

GOOD PRACTICE ▷ *Contact the public enquiry sector of the Health and Safety Executive, at Rose Court, Southwark Bridge Road, London SE1 9HF (Tel.: 0171 717 6000) to receive all published material relating to health and safety.*

In salon entertainment

Many hairdressing and beauty salons play background music within their establishments to create the appropriate type of ambience. In beauty and health clinics it is often intended to create a relaxing environment whereas the environment of the hair salon is much more lively. If the owner decides to play recorded music they will need to pay a fee whereas if they use a television or radio broadcasts they will need to buy a licence.

POINT TO NOTE ▷

For information on current fees contact:

Performing Rights Society Ltd, 29–33 Berners Street, London W1V 4 AA
Tel. 0171 580 5544

Phonographic Performance Ltd, Ganton House, 14–22 Ganton Street, London W1V 1LB
Tel. 0171 437 0311

POINT TO NOTE ▷

The EU directive to list product ingredients became effective on 1st January 1997. However, companies have until 31st December 1997 to sell any existing stock.

KEY TERMS

You need to know what these words and phrases mean. Go back through the chapter to find out.

Employment legislation	Disability discrimination
Fire precautions	Disciplinary procedures
COSHH	Termination of employment
The 'six pack'	Unfair dismissal
Sex discrimination	Treatment and consumer legislation

5 Marketing and promotion

This chapter covers the following areas:
- ➤ corporate image
- ➤ marketing
- ➤ costing of services
- ➤ advertising, promotion and publicity
- ➤ marketing strategies.

Many owners may wonder why business is not better when they feel they are offering an excellent service, using top quality products and employing well qualified and highly competent staff. The answer will generally lie in the fact that they are not marketing themselves sufficiently.

Marketing is not just about placing an advertisement in the local paper, it is the whole product, the image that the salon wishes to create. In the business of aesthetics this is never more important; attention to detail counts. Marketing your services to the right audience requires foresight, empathy, knowledge, enthusiasm and above all understanding.

POINT TO NOTE ▷ *Marketing drives business. It is considered to be the process by which the planning, conception, promotion and distribution of services and goods satisfy the objectives of the individual and organisation.*

Corporate image

A corporate image is essential to all business as it provides a direct visual image of the business to the consumer. It will depend upon the type and size of the business as to the type of image they wish to project, e.g. reliable, supportive, creative, traditional, modern. Corporate identity is seen as the particular image that a company wishes to project, to existing and potential consumers, and this is most effectively conveyed in visual terms. Careful planning of everything to do with the company and its products/services is needed to ensure that the company will be instantly recognisable. This generally involves the use of a logo (such as a lettering style or font which is displayed on the top of a shop, side of a vehicle or letter head etc.) or a visual symbol which will be identifiable, either on a conscious or subconscious level, as that particular company. The keynote to corporate identity is consistency so it is essential that the business owner identifies everything they will use and need for their business, e.g.

- letterhead
- business card
- appointment card
- newsletter
- brochure
- advertisements
- job advertisements
- application forms
- company handbook
- shop front and window display
- uniforms.

Larger companies may also need to consider the use of motor vehicles, video or television advertisements etc.

It may well be that small business want to use the logo of their professional association as this will be more widely recognised by potential clients as a sign of quality and reassurance. Larger businesses may wish to encompass this logo with their own.

Fig. 5.1 *Examples of corporate identity within the health, beauty and hairdressing professions*

Having established all the material that the salon may use at one time or another the next step is to recruit a graphic designer or design agency to establish possible costs. The graphic designer or design agency will quote for the design concepts, artwork materials and print costs. It must be remembered that these costs will vary depending on a number of factors, i.e. the size and reputation of the designer or agency, the quality of the paper selected and the number of colours to be used (the more colours involved the higher the print costs will be). The owner also needs to give serious consideration as to the quantities of the items that will be used as the quantity of the print run will affect the cost. They also need to establish the price for any print reruns that they might need.

POINT TO NOTE ▷   *The price for design will obviously vary from designer to designer so it is important to obtain a number of quotes. Shop around from a small company, a high street reprographic centre, a design centre within a college to a large design agency.*

Marketing

In today's world marketing is needed more than ever due to the wide variety of choice that clients have. Marketing can be seen as 'demand creation' which basically means you have to create a demand for what you offer. It is essential that consideration is given to the services and products offered as no matter how good these are, unless their is a need for them they are useless. The owner of the business must identify the benefits and features of what they are actually selling, along with the client need for these, in order to be successful.

The marketing mix

The traditional foundation to start the marketing process is the marketing mix, which is commonly referred to as 'the four Ps':

- product
- price
- place
- promotion.

However, more recent research has indicated that this foundation requiresthe addition of a further two points, namely:

- quality
- customer service.

These six points are all equal in their importance to successful marketing so an emphasis should not be placed on any one of them.

Quality and customer service

Quality and customer service must be reflected in everything the business does and offers, including the performance, appearance etc. of all the staff. They should not be seen as extras offered but as an integral part of the business because without these the business can not effectively compete with other establishments or individuals.

Products

Product is used to refer to the services and products offered by the business to the client in exchange for payment. It also includes the image that the owner projects to the clients of the business, the salon and their staff.

Careful consideration must be given to ensure that the services and products used by the business will be marketable. There must be a need or demand for the service or product because without this there will be no business. When taking on new treatments or products the owner must ensure that they select ones that meet their client needs and that the staff are able to deliver these to the best of their ability.

GOOD PRACTICE ▷

- *Keep separate records on new products or services; keep only those that meet the customer needs and the goals of the business.*
- *It is important to remember that products and services, like people, have a life cycle (birth, growth, maturity, old age, death) and that a careful check must be kept on this to ensure that they continue to reflect current market demands.*

Price

Price refers to the actual cost that the owner sets on the services or products of the business. It is essential to set this correctly as the price will reflect how successful the business will be. If the owner does not estimate correctly the costs of the treatment and allow a suitable profit margin the business will lose money and cease to be viable, whereas if treatments are overpriced the client may go elsewhere so the business once again loses out. The costs charged by competitors must also be borne in mind along with the present economic climate.

Costing of services

Many salons do not properly cost out their services so therefore they do not make an adequate profit and wonder why the business is not doing very well even though the appointment book is always full! Costing is very important and should encompass fixed, variable and depreciation costs along with the potential business sales as these will affect the profit made.

- Fixed costs are the permanent outgoing costs of the business no matter what services are provided or in what quantity. They include such items as rent, business and water rates, national insurance payments and insurance premiums.

- Variable costs are the business outgoings that may alter from day to day, week to week or month to month (according to the method of book keeping used) depending on the quantity and type of service provided to clients. These will include such items as materials used, labour costs, advertisements, printing costs, postage costs, travel costs, telephone, heating and lighting costs etc.

● Depreciation costs are related only to the major purchases of a business such as equipment, computers, cars etc. These items are considered to be fixed assets of the business and can be offset against the accounts of the business for taxation purposes.

Manicure treatment (30 minutes)		**£12.00**
Fixed costs		£ 1.50
Variable costs:	Materials	£ 0.50
	Electricity	£ 0.60
	Laundry	£ 0.90
	Miscellaneous	£ 0.50
	Labour	£ 4.00
Sub-total		£ 8.00
Profit @ 50%		£ 4.00
Total charge		£12.00

Notes:

● The quarterly fixed costs, e.g. rent, are divided by the number of hours to give an hourly rate and then divided again by the number of practitioners.

● The figures for the materials are obtained by dividing how much the product would cost at retail by the number of times that you can use the product.

● The electricity, laundry and miscellaneous (variable costs, e.g printing, marketing etc.) costs are calculated by taking the quarterly bills, dividing them by the number of hours to find the hourly rate and then dividing again by the number of practitioners.

● Labour in this instance is calculated on thebasis of the practitioner working for £8.00 per hour.

● Profit is calculated on 50% of the total costs.

Aromatherapy treatment (90 minutes)		**£35.25**
Fixed costs		£ 4.50
Variable costs:	Materials	£ 1.00
	Electricity	£ 1.80
	Laundry	£ 2.70
	Miscellaneous	£ 1.50
	Labour	£12.00
Sub-total		£23.50
Profit @ 50%		£11.75
Total charge		£35.25

Permanent wave (150 minutes) £57.90

Labour in this example is calculated on a stylist working for one hour @ £8.00 per hour and a junior working for one and a half hours @ £4.00 per hour, giving a total labour cost of £14.00.

Fixed costs		£ 7.50
Variable costs:	Materials	£ 6.50
	Electricity	£ 3.60
	Laundry	£ 4.50
	Miscellaneous	£ 2.50
	Labour	£14.00
Sub-total		£38.60
Profit @ 50%		£19.30
Total charge		£57.90

Fig. 5.2 *Examples of costings of treatments within the health, beauty and hairdressing industries*

Variable costs are generally affected by the number and type of services provided, e.g. if a beauty salon performs eight body massages on one day and two on another the amount of massage oil used, heating required and the quantity of towels needing to be laundered will be higher on one day than another, so these variable costs will fluctuate dependent on services performed.

Cost is the value of something that the business has used, whereas capital is the value of something that the business owns, e.g. if a business purchases £2000 worth of products at the beginning of a month and uses up £1500 by the end of the month, then the business costs on products are £1500 and the business capital on products is £500.

ACTIVITY

Research and review:

(a) acceptable market prices for treatments offered in a city centre, high profile salon or clinic

(b) whether the market will allow the salon or clinic to charge varying rates such as at busy or quiet times or periods

(c) whether the market segment expects varying rates, e.g for children, old age pensioners etc.

Place

Place is used to refer to the channels of distribution used by the business, the opening hours, scheduling and purchases of materials. It encompasses the mechanisms used to ensure that the services and products are easily available to clients and the routes by which the salon obtains its products. The owner must establish client confidence in the availability of the services when and where they want them. Careful consideration needs to be given to the location and opening hours of the business.

GOOD PRACTICE ▷ *Display the services offered, prices and opening times in the window to highlight the cost and availability to 'window shoppers' or passers by.*

Advertising, promotion and publicity

Advertising, promotion and publicity includes all the steps that the owner takes to inform clients of the services and products of the business in order to persuade clients to purchase them. It includes all the communication tools that can be used in marketing, e.g. personal selling, advertising, sales promotion, publicity, telephone sales, direct marketing etc.

POINT TO NOTE ▷ *In the planning of any new business it is important to ensure a good marketing mix. Consider the following:*

- *develop products and services*
- *ensure that all products and services provide quality and client value*
- *set the prices for these services and products*
- *make the services and products available*
- *identify to whom they will be sold*
- *inform clients of these services and products*
- *encourage clients to purchase them*
- *satisfy client needs*
- *make sure the clients return.*

SWOT *analysis*

It is essential for an existing business or potential new one to identify its strengths, weaknesses, opportunities and threats (SWOT) to enable the owner to enhance or develop the business to its maximum capacity. The analysis enables the business owner to develop a clear picture from thorough research of their potential market and their competitors. It is also paramount that careful research and consideration should be been given to the finances available and possible financial sources, e.g. Prince's Trust, European Social Fund etc.

Examples of some possible strengths

- Individual staff
- The team of specialist staff offering complementary services
- Specialist or unique skills offered
- Specialist or unique products offered
- Location of the business
- Ambience of the business
- Free car parking
- Team and personal support
- Opening hours etc.

Examples of some possible weaknesses

- Staff personalities
- Individual staff
- Lack of experience
- Lack of support
- Skills offered
- Products used
- Location of the business
- Ambience of the business
- No car parking
- Opening hours etc.

Examples of some potential opportunities
- Expansion
- Introduction of new staff, skills, products etc.
- Financial support perhaps through government schemes etc.
- Social and economic changes

Examples of some potential threats
- Competitors
- Availability of products, staff etc.
- Social and economic changes

Business forecast

To enable the owner to plan for any marketing of their business they must first of all research information that may assist in identifying their current position, the positions of their competitors and any gaps in the market. To provide this data they should clarify the following:

- what their business is about
- how they perceive the business
- what are its strengths and weaknesses
- what is the size of the available market
- who are the potential clients
- what are the demographics of these clients
- what motivates these clients to actually buy
- who are the competitors
- how many competitors are there
- where are the competitors' businesses located
- what services and products do these competitors offer
- what prices do these competitors charge for their services and products
- what can these competitors offer that they can't
- who are the competitors' clients
- what can the owner offer the clients that the competitors can't
- what external factors are affecting the business, e.g. economics, current and future treatment trends, technological advances etc.

POINT TO NOTE ▷

There are many external factors that affect business operations and these are the factors which influence the business environment:

Economic climate	*Financial implications on costs and expenditure*
Social trends	*Implications of current lifestyle trends, education standards and client knowledge, awareness, age, gender and culture trends or issues etc.*
Political trends	*Government and local legislation or regulations*
Natural environment	*Health and safety issues, 'environmentally friendly' issues etc.*
Technological trends	*Technological advances, new products, services, equipment etc.*
Competitive trends	*Marketing potential of one business over another*

Once the owner has addressed all of the above the information gathered must be analysed thoroughly and conclusions drawn. In today's modern world a computer may be used to record, analyse and draw conclusions on all of this information which makes for a much easier and quicker process than in yeas gone by. The data provided from this research will provide the owner with a business forecast (the viability and longevity of the business) by identifying the current business position and the strategies needed to enable the owner to create a demand for the services and products offered at the present time or in the future. It will also form the foundation for the marketing plan.

GOOD PRACTICE ▷ *When carrying out a SWOT analysis, always establish the link between the strengths and opportunities and the threats and weaknesses. Then establish what can be done to market the strengths and eliminate the weaknesses.*

POINT TO NOTE ▷ *Never underestimate the effect the economy can have on a service industry. Use marketing tactics to survive times of recession, e.g alter prices of services, offer 'specials' such as a free manicure with a perm.*

Marketing plan

Planning is the essence of a successful business. It takes research time, analytical skills and forward planning to aim for and achieve goals so the marketing plan is crucial. In years gone by marketing was often considered a separate area of the business whereas today it is considered an integral role. In the past the concept was to focus on the product whereas now the client is considered essential to the business and therefore the most important thing to consider. Every aspect of the business must be viewed through the eyes of the client as only the client can decide whether or not they have received value for money.

The key principle in current marketing trends is to 'satisfy the client's needs' and therefore quality and service must be the pivot for the marketing plan to maintain existing clients' happiness and business and to attract new clients to the business.

POINT TO NOTE ▷ *It is essential to differentiate between the services of the business and their features. The service is what is offered and its features are its identifiable attributes.*

GOOD PRACTICE ▷ *Involve the staff team in the marketing process by drawing on their experience and ideas. Encourage them to think about and aim for the success of the business. Instil in them the desire to provide each of the business customers with value for money.*

ACTIVITY

Identify three services within your service sector and list the features of each to potential clients. An example of a service within the beauty salon is a facial and its features will include such things as cleansing the skin, performing a lymph drainage massage and applying a hydrating face mask; it will improve the client's skin condition and aid in their relaxation and sense of well being.
An example of a service within the haidressing salon is a conditioning treatment and its features will include such things as cleansing the hair, performing a scalp massage and applying a hydrating, nourishing conditioner; it will improve the client's hair condition and aid in their relaxation and sense of well being.

Client base

The business needs to develop the loyalty of the clients in order to retain them. Establishing a suitable client base, according to the quantity of resources such as staff and treatment areas, is the key to achieving a successful business. The loyalty needs to be to the business not to a particular practitioner otherwise as practitioners leave so will the clients!

GOOD PRACTICE ▷ *Encourage clients through staff to have treatments from a number of practitioners. This is useful for client confidence when a practitioner is off ill or leaves the business. It takes clients time to build up trust and feel confident in a different practitioner but if they have gradually adjusted to treatment with a few this problem is alleviated.*

Marketing strategies

Mass and micro marketing

Micro marketing is growing in popularity today and is steadily replacing the concept of mass marketing whereby the whole market was targeted in one way to address everyone. It is very apparent that micro marketing has distinctive major advantages in that it targets different segments, e.g. different ranges of clients requiring different services. Obviously by segmenting your marketing plan costs may be higher than if one overall mechanism was to be used. For example, a hairdressing and beauty salon may identify through research and development that the requirements of clients in one area of the business are very different to those of the clients in the other area. They may specialise in teenage hair trends in the hairdressing salon but in the beauty salon they specialise in stress - elated treatments, and therefore need to target their marketing accordingly.

Forms of advertising and promotion

Direct marketing is becoming much more widely used as social lifestyles have created active and often hectic lifestyles reducing time available to potential clients to shop or window shop. The last decade has seen a great increase in the use of home shopping whether by catalogue, television or 'doorstep'. It has also seen a growth in the number of home visiting or mobile practitioners.

POINT TO NOTE ▷

Markets can be split into different segments of demographic data to assist target marketing. For example, people (the market) may be studied and categorised by:

- *gender*
- *age*
- *marital status*
- *role theory (e.g. mother, sister, wife, employer, employee)*
- *location/type of housing*
- *social class*
- *economic situation*
- *employment/occupation*
- *leisure activities*
- *where they shop.*

ACTIVITY

Research the different segments that could be used for collating market data for:

(a) a well-established large city centre practice

(b) a new small suburban practice.

Lifestyle marketing means using statistical data on people's lifestyles, such as where they live, where they shop, how they spend their leisure time. The social and economic climate will affect people's lifestyles so the successful business will keep abreast of these changes and market accordingly. The last decade has seen an enormous growth in the number of working women so businesses have had to adapt such things as their opening hours (opening prior to and after office hours) to accommodate the lifestyle changes in this segment of the market.

POINT TO NOTE ▷

● *Statistics indicate that the UK has an ageing population and that by the year 2040, eighty per cent of the population will be pensioners.*

● *Service expectations vary widely across age spans, e.g. a teenager's view of quality service will vary from that of a mature adult.*

ACTIVITY

1 Analyse the service expectations for your industry sector of the following age ranges:
   (a) 16–20 year olds
   (b) 20–25 year olds
   (c) 25–35 year olds
   (d) 35–45 year olds
   (e) 45–55 year olds
   (f) 55 +

2 Draw up a comparison chart between groups (a) and (f).

3 List an action plan to address the expectations of an ageing population.

Other marketing strategies of the 1990s include environmental marketing to meet the consumers' growing awareness of their natural environment and the detrimental effect that products can have on it, e.g. product manufacturers have developed more natural ingredients, biodegradable packaging etc. All of these things can attract this segment of the market to use your services. Another growing strategy is advocacy marketing which uses causes as a way of attracting customers, such as subsidising a charity through sales on certain things or by promotion of causes, e.g. using products that are not tested on animals to support animal rights groups.

Advertising

Having identified the needs of the different market segments the owner of the business is able to match the appropriate services to these needs and cost them correctly to ensure the business will establish a profit. The next stage is to formulate an advertising and promotional plan that will fit into the budget. Advertising does require money

There are a large varieties of ways in which the owner can advertise and promote the business. The cost will vary depending on the form being used and it can often be influenced by the area of the country the business is located in. The key points to remember having established the service needs of the business and market are to use advertising and promotion to:

1 Attract clients' attention
Ensure that your advert will stand out; consider carefully its layout, design, use of graphics, colour and typography to make your point.

2 Maintain their interest
It is important that an advert uses a powerful message to retain the prospective clients' interest.

3 Create a desire
Having attracted their attention and maintained their interest the next step is to ensure the mechanisms used create a desire within the client for the service.

4 Take action
The final process that the advertisement should create is for the client to take up the services promoted.

GOOD PRACTICE ▷ *It is essential to establish the objectives of the advertisement prior to designing it. For example, is it to:*

- *promote new services or products*
- *re-attract old clients*
- *reassure clients*
- *improve the company profile*
- *back up previous advertisements*
- *inform potential clients how successful the business is*
- *establish a new business*
- *help build client loyalty?*

POINTS TO NOTE ▷ *Advertising is a method of communicating the business services, that have been determined through the marketing analysis, to the clients who will be attracted to them. As with all communication the message must be clear to the people the business wants to reach.*

Forms of advertising
The main forms of advertising are:
- link advertising with a complementary business, e.g. a health food shop promoting the services of a natural health clinic and vice versa or a hairdressing salon linking with a beauty salon or a doctors' surgery linking with a chiropractic surgery etc.
- business cards
- word of mouth
- advertising in local shops
- telephone sales
- advertising in local newspapers/magazines
- advertising in national newspapers/magazines
- circulars/newsletters/promotional leaflets
- advertising on the exterior of business vehicles

- advertising on the interior or exterior of buses or taxis
- advertising on wall planners , calendars, diary etc.
- Yellow Pages
- billboard advertising
- radio
- television.

Fig. 5.3 *Examples of business cards*

ACTIVITY

List the advantages and disadvantages to a small suburban and home visiting/mobile practitioner of the different forms of advertising available.

Promotions

Promotion of services or products tends to involve offering some kind of discount on the service or product. For example, clients are often offered a discount if they book and pay in advance for a course of treatments. This tends to be offered to entice a client to outlay a reasonable sum of money and in the past this was considered a good way of ensuring that they would keep their appointments. However, many owners find that today this is often not the case and can lead to more difficulties fitting these clients in when they cancel or try to make last minute bookings. If this type of promotion is used it must be carefully planned to reflect

Fig. 5.4 *Examples of Yellow Pages corporate advertising*

the resources of the business. Discounted trial treatments are offered in many beauty salons to encourage clients to try new services. Often sales companies will send a member of their staff to assist the salon in promoting the service. Another type of promotion is to offer a discounted or free treatment when a client purchases a certain treatment, e.g. a free manicure with a perm. Alternatively a voucher redeemable against services during a quiet period of the year may be offered, e.g. a voucher sent to existing clients redeemable against treatments over a certain value during an eight-week period after Christmas.

Before deciding on any promotions it is important to establish:

● what is the aim of the promotion

● do you need to offer it

● what are the benefits to the business of the promotion

● what will it cost you?

It makes good business sense to ensure that a promotion is worthwhile to the business before undertaking it. It is extremely important for the success of the business that any advertising and promotion of the business is monitored, reviewed and amended accordingly.

ACTIVITY

Research twenty different promotional ideas that would be applicable to your industry sector and benefit your business.

POINT TO NOTE ▷ *The two most common reasons for offering promotions within the hair and beauty sectors are to introduce new services or staff and to reduce excess capacity, e.g. stock due to pass its sell by date or staff with little to do in slack periods.*

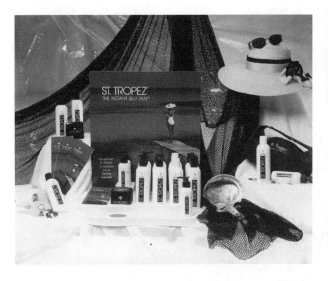 

Fig. 5.5 *Examples of promotional displays*

GOOD PRACTICE ▷
- Use reception areas and windows to highlight promotional offers.
- Investigate which product or equipment distributors offer marketing and promotion support to their salons.
- Research the marketing benefits of being a member of a professional association.

POINTS TO NOTE ▷
- Product and equipment distributors often offer a great deal of support on marketing and promotions which are extremely cost effective for the small business. It is often cheaper to buy gift vouchers etc from them than it is to have them printed yourself.
- Professional associations may offer different marketing services to their members, e.g. promoting public awareness of the professionalism of their members and issuing membership information free to potential clients etc.
- Trade journals may publish salon names and addresses free within a directory of salon services.

GOOD PRACTICE ▷

● *Client record cards or computerised systems can be used to collate data on where the client heard about the salon or service. This ensures that only successful mechanisms are re-used.*

● *Surveys are a useful way of gaining data on existing clients' views on how the business and its services can be improved.*

● *If the business has a ground floor window, eye-catching displays can be used to promote the business. However, it is important that these don't remain stagnant!*

Publicity

Publicity is the acclaim the business achieves whether it is beneficial or detrimental. One of the best forms of publicity any business can achieve is through word of mouth. So it is essential that the client is happy with the quality and service of the business.

Fig. 5.6 *Trade magazine salon directory*

ACTIVITY

1   Perform a SWOT analysis on a business.

2   Investigate the costs for a range of forms of advertising and
    decide which methods are most suitable for:
    (a) a home visiting/mobile practitioner
    (b) a small suburban practice
    (c) a large city centre practice which is part of a major group.

3   Investigate the marketing support offered by each of the
    following:
    (a) professional associations
    (b) product and equipment distributors
    (c) trade journals.

KEY TERMS

*You need to know what these
words and phrases mean. Go
back through the chapter to find
out.*

Corporate identity
Marketing
Quality and customer service
Costing of services

Advertising
Promotion and publicity
SWOT analysis

6 Management theories and style

This chapter covers the following areas:
- ➤ the importance of theories
- ➤ organisational theory
- ➤ motivation theories
- ➤ leadership theories
- ➤ communication mechanisms
- ➤ team roles
- ➤ practical and effective management techniques.

The importance of theories

In order for a theory to be useful it must be supported by some form of evidence which may at the time the theories are made vary in strength and acceptability. For example, Charles Darwin's 'theory of evolution' was supported by observational evidence of natural phenomena and described by imaginative construct. At the time his evidence was weak and he was ridiculed by the majority of his colleagues, religious activists and the general public. However, as time has elapsed the number of people opposing his theory has lessened and it has been accepted by many as making perfect sense.

Theories are often represented in paradigms (model form) illustrating an individual's or group of people's ideas.

Organisational theory

Management theory is more modernly referred to as organisational theory, i.e. the ability to organise yourself, your staff and your colleagues.

Charles Handy defines organisation theory as follows:

'helps one to explain the past which, in turn helps one to understand the future which leads to more influence over future events and to suffer less disturbances from the unexpected'.

One of the pioneers in management psychology during the mid-1950s was A.H. Maslow who put forward the theory that there are five basic needs that people aim to satisfy:

1 Self-fulfilment
The need to feel content with oneself.

2 Esteem
The individual's need to have status and respect from others.

3 Social
The importance of an individual's acceptance by others.

110

Fig. 6.1 *Charles Darwin (1809–1882)*

4 Safety
The individual's need to feel secure, protected, to have continuity.

5 Physiological
The basic need for food, clothes and shelter.

These points can be viewed as a pyramid (see Fig. 6.2) building upon the physiological needs which are considered to be the most basic, leading to self-fulfilment which is considered to be the pinnacle for which all people aim.

Motivation theories

The definition of motivity is power of moving or of producing motion so we can use motivation to refer to making something move or do something. It is used in 'management speak' to encourage staff to work, making them interested enough in their job to take part in it, perform tasks and hopefully gain personal satisfaction from it. The historical perception of motivation assumes a number of things about human beings:

- they are rational, economic beings motivated by their own needs

- they are social beings who are happier functioning as a team

- they are self-fulfilling beings who motivate themselves

- they are complex beings who can be unpredictable in their response to management strategies

- they are psychological beings who strive towards their image of themselves.

Fig. 6.2 *Maslow's hierarchy of needs*

After a great deal of research organisational theorists have developed a formula for motivation based on the 'E' factors:

- Effort
- Enthusiasm
- Energy
- Excitement
- Expenditure
- Effectiveness
- Efficiency.

It is the role of the manager to activate as many 'E' factors in their staff as possible. It is important to remember that all employees have a psychological contract with their employer, organisation or their job. We all have many psychological contracts with people we don't want to let down, e.g. our family, sports or social clubs; such is human nature.

Psychological contracts can be useful for motivating staff providing they are:

- more satisfying in the employee's eyes than any other contract they are currently holding. Job motivation does not generally compete well with a wedding, a new baby or moving house so allowances need to be made for personal events of major importance in an employee's life.
- identically viewed by the employee and organisation, as the contract can then be depended upon by both sides, becoming predictable and useful.

Fig. 6.3 'E' *factors*

Psychological contracts can be perceived as three different types:

- **coercive** – using the fear of punishment to bring forth the 'E' factors; this is commonly known as the 'stick' approach.
- **calculative** – using some sort of reward as the 'carrot' to bring forth the 'E' factors; this reward is often more money or time off.
- **co-operative** – using leadership skills, or the needs of the organisation or task to be undertaken to bring forth the 'E' factors. With this type of contract the employee must identify closely with the needs of the organisation (the phenomena of the company person and the vocational calling).

It is impossible to force a co-operative contract on an employee, they must pick it up themselves; it is like responsibility it cannot be given, it has to be taken.

ACTIVITY

1   In a small group brainstorm the notion of 'E' factors; see how many more you can think of.
2   Think of a group of people you know – a staff team. How many 'E' factors can you attribute to each member of the team?
3   Think of three different types of groups to which you belong, e.g. professional association, parent teachers association, church etc. Then answer the following:
    (a) (i)   What do these groups expect from you?
        (ii) What do you expect from the group?
    (b) List their expectations in order of importance to (i) yourself and (ii) the group.
    (c) List your expectations in order of importance to (i) yourself and (ii) the group.
4   What do the answers to the above tell you about the psychological contracts you have with these groups?

I'm sure these have got a lot further away!

Fig. 6.4 *'Carrot' motivation*

Traditional motivation theories

There are thought to be three traditional motivation theories:

1 Satisfaction motivation theory, whereby the workers' mere passive satisfaction equals their productivity.

2 Incentive motivation theory, where rewards are given to bring forth 'E' factors, thus resulting in more productivity.

3 Intrinsic motivation theory, where in the opinion of the worker the job is considered worthwhile in its own right and therefore brings forth 'E' factors resulting in more productivity.

Herzberg's two-factor theory of motivation

An idea to explain what motivates people was put forward by the American theorist Herzberg and it became known as the 'two- factor theory of motivation'. His theory was based on interviews and question-naires and incorporated existing theories. Herzberg identified two factors at work which can cause satisfaction (known as satisfiers or motivators) or dissatisfaction (known as dissatisfiers or maintenance). These factors do not oppose each other so changing a dissatisfier will not change it into a satisfying or motivating factor. Herzberg claimed that the division of the two factors answers two questions, namely 'Why work harder?' and 'Why work here?'(see Fig. 6.5).

Principles of scientific management – Taylor

Taylor identified and described a number of factors which could be seen to influence successful staff performance. These mainly highlighted the fact that staff were motivated by money or economic factors. His ideas are reflected in many of the staff bonus schemes in operation today, e.g. performance related pay, commission etc.

Why work harder? **Motivational factors** (Satisfiers) Recognition Achievement Responsibility Advancement	Why work here? **Maintenance factors** (Dissatisfiers) Salary Conditions Policies Interpersonal relationships

Fig. 6.5 *Herzberg's two-factor theory of motivation*

Hawthorne studies

Research undertaken in the late 1920s to analyse the effects of a large variety of factors that influence work output (such as lighting, supervision and rest breaks), highlighted that individual staff's motivation was affected by the staff team. The effect of this team on the individual's motivation could either be a positive or negative influence. These studies produced information on why people work harder and they also gave rise to an analytical tool known as the 'Hawthorne effect' which requests that whenever observational studies are made that allowance should be made if the subjects of the study are aware that they are being observed. As an outcome of this study a great deal of observational work is undertaken by disguised participating researchers or through a two-way mirror.

GOOD PRACTICE ▷

The Hawthorne studies clearly identify:

- *the importance of ensuring that all staff are aware of their value to the organisation*
- *that staff work harder if someone takes an interest in their work.*

Psychological theory of the locus of control

In 1966 Rotter originally described this theory, which has been highlighted further by Rubin and McNeil in 1983, that human beings need to be in control of their own life. This theory indicates that some people feel that they are influenced by external factors (external locus of control) in their life, e.g. knowing the right person to get a good job, being in the right place at the right time, 'it's not what you know but who you know', 'some people are born lucky'. Others are influenced by internal factors (internal locus of control) which are a result of their own efforts, such as not obtaining a job because they performed badly at interview, not achieving an examination pass as they didn't study hard enough etc. This study showed that those people who have an internal locus of control will work harder and are generally more successful than those with an external locus of control.

POINT TO NOTE ▷

It is useful for a manager to identify whether each of their staff members has an internal or external locus of control.

ACTIVITY

1 Reflect on your own life and identify times when you were prevented from progression by psychological needs.

2 Consider the team of people you work with or who work for you and identify whether they:
expect rewards from hard work
expect rewards from factors of good luck.

NACH (*need to achieve*) – McClelland

McClelland's research noted that some people are extremely motivated by their individual need to be successful or achieve something in their life. This need is not found in everyone and can be influenced by culture as some cultures instil in their children the importance in life of achieving (being successful).

Individuals who are motivated by achievement set themselves targets, strive towards them and need feedback on their progress. McClelland noted that the need to achieve can be learnt by using four key points:

1 Teaching individuals to talk, think and act achievement.

2 Stimulating individuals to set well-structured targets.

3 Helping individuals to develop an awareness of themselves.

4 Creating a team spirit to enable the team to share their desires, successes, failures and fears.

GOOD PRACTICE ▷ *Use the four key points highlighted by McClelland to help build a motivated team.*

ERG *theory – Alderfer*

In recent years Alderfer has developed the ERG (existence, relatedness and growth) theory which is a three-factor need theory. It relates closely to the hierarchy of needs theory developed by Maslow in that basic needs must first be addressed and satisfied before any of the higher level needs are met. Three important points are highlighted by Alderfer:

1 The less a need is satisfied then the more important this need becomes.

2 The more a lower level need is satisfied then the greater the importance of the next level need will be.

3 The less a higher level need is satisfied then the greater the importance of the lower level need will be.

It is important to note from Alderfer's three-factor need theory that employees may become demanding and often disruptive if they cannot get what they want from a job. They will often demand more of what they can get to try and compensate for their needs not being addressed, e.g. an employee who needs a challenge in their job may become frustrated by the lack of challenge and demand more money to compensate for the higher level need not being met.

Vroom's expectancy (instrumentality) theory

This theory is based on an individual's process of decision-making skills and the logistics of choice as a motivator, e.g in order for performance related pay to be effective the individual has to think that the effort of additional work is worth the additional money it will give and of course the individual must want the additional money! There are basically two factors the individual has to consider:

- preference – how much they want the outcome which is on offer or available to them
- expectancy – how much effort is needed to achieve the outcome.

POINTS TO NOTE ▷ *Managers should consider the expectancy theory when designing systems, in particular the following points:*

(a) in order for a reward to be worthwhile employees expect to put in effort

(b) employees must believe that the results will bring the reward

(c) employees must want the reward enough to put in the required effort.

Goldthorpe's affluent worker in the class structure theory

This is not a well-established theory but it indicates that for many people work is simply a means to an end. The job itself is not particularly important, only the pay which enables them to do what they really want to, e.g. socialise, raise a family etc.

GOOD PRACTICE ▷ *Where an employee is not motivated by job satisfaction but only by money and time off, use time of in lieu as a reward for hard work to motivate them. A single parent or parent of a school-aged child may be more motivated by working school hours and being able to take holidays in line with those of their child.*

POINT TO NOTE ▷ *A motivated workforce is a productive one.*

McKinsey's seven S's theory

This theory emphasises the connection between the role and tasks of a manager. The seven S's are:

● shared values
● structure of the business and how it operates
● systems within the business, such as record keeping
● style, e.g. suitable leadership style for the business
● staff motivation and support
● skills needed within the business
● strategy or plans for the business.

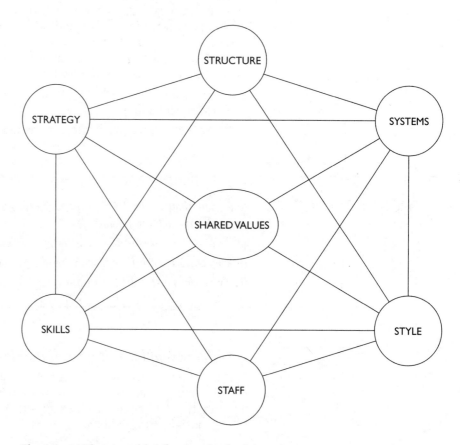

Fig. 6.6 *McKinsey's model of the role and tasks of the manager*

ACTIVITY

Research further and discuss the relevance of the following theories and consider their outcomes on motivating a workforce:

● the psychological theory of the locus of control (Rother, 1966)
● Herzberg's two-factor theory of motivation (1966, 1968)
● Alderfer's ERG theory
● McKinsey's seven S's.

Non-traditional motivation theories

1 Job enrichment

This is sometimes known as job enhancement and is a technique that may be used to make a job appear more rewarding or interesting to the employee.

2 Open book management

An engineering company from America pioneered this concept of motivation in the 1990s. Regular meetings for all staff are held explaining the business processes and access to accounts etc.

3 Quality circles

This approach to motivation was first established in Japan before being adopted in the 1980s by America and Europe. The concept of the quality circle is to motivate individuals through involvement in decision making and then feeding back and reinforcing positive outcomes.

Fig. 6.7 *A quality circle meeting*

POINT TO NOTE ▷

The real motivators are considered to be:

- *achievement – the majority of people want the satisfaction of actually making a meaningful contribution*
- *recognition – it is natural that employees want recognition for their efforts*
- *advancement – the majority of employees want to move on to new challenges*
- *responsibility – most skilled employees are very happy to accept responsibility*
- *interest – the opportunity to show intelligence in the workplace or practice a skill motivates employees.*

ACTIVITY   List the points that you consider to be motivating factors in your job.

Leadership theories

There are a variety of views on what constitutes a leader and how someone can become a good leader. Clarification of leadership is difficult to achieve but what certainly has been identified are three main ways of looking at what makes a good leader:

1 The trait theory

This theory recommends that there are lists of different traits (qualities) that make a good leader, e.g. enthusiasm, warmth, calmness, integrity etc. The traits required will obviously be dependent on the situation and job remit.

2 Leadership style theory

In this theory leaders are divided into the following types.

Autocrat

This type of leader acts on their own, making all the decisions on the running of the business and will tell employees what they have to do. It tends to be a style that demotivates staff and prevents team building.

Democrat

This style of leadership will involve listening to the views of others before making any decisions. It will therefore involve staff, encourage team participation and motivate the work force unless the team need a great deal of support in participating in and reaching decisions.

Activity/task leader

This type of leader is one who concentrates on the task in hand at the time, putting all their efforts into that particular job.

Consultative leader

This type of leader encourages team participation but will make the final decisions themselves.

People leader

This style of leader tends to care more about their actual staff in terms of their emotions etc. than the other types of leaders would.

Laissez faire leader

This type of leader intervenes as little as possible, so the team tend towards becoming leaderless.

3 The contingency model

This style refers to adapting the approach needed at the time to fit the task, situation or team needs.

POINTS TO NOTE ▷ *Appointing the right manager for the business is essential if the business is to be a success.*

Communication mechanisms

A clear constructive system of communication is essential within all businesses in order to pass and retrieve information on structures, systems, products and equipment. It is required to monitor and evaluate the strengths and weaknesses of the business and most importantly for the business to gain and maintain clients.

POINTS TO NOTE ▷
- *Never allow staff to shout across a room to a colleague.*
- *Ensure that all staff are conscious of the ambience required within the business and that they work towards enhancing this not destroying it.*
- *Ensure that staff never disturb a holistic practitioner whilst treatment is in progress.*
- *Within a hairdressing salon always ensure the staff excuse themselves to the client before speaking to the stylist.*

The owner or manager will obviously need to have excellent personal and interpersonal skills and to establish clear systems of communication. They must ensure that all staff are trained in these systems and that they are closely monitored to ensure that they are effective. This will include:

- telephone answering technique, e.g Good morning, the Natural Health Clinic, John speaking, how may I help you?
- method for making clients' appointments and recording these in the appointment book
- taking and recording messages
- recording income and expenditure
- greeting and receiving clients
- addressing and conversing with other practitioners within the business
- staff meetings
- recruiting new staff
- interview methods
- advertising the staff and services of the business
- receiving, recording and monitoring stock
- monitoring and appraising staff.

GOOD PRACTICE ▷

- Hold regular staff meetings.
- Record the items discussed and the action to be taken.
- Make it clear who is expected to take the action.
- Always follow through the notes of the previous meeting to ensure action has been appropriately addressed.
- Praise examples of good work at these meetings.
- Introduce an employee of the month award; involve the staff in setting the criteria and the staff and clients in judging it.
- Create interest, enthusiasm and team work.
- Address issues concerning the staff and business.
- Ensure all staff feel able to contribute.
- Listen to their point of view.
- Don't allow anyone to dominate the meeting.
- Create warmth and understanding among the staff when handling a problem between them.

Fig. 6.8   Examples of body language in meetings: (**a**) disinterested; (**b**) active participation.

ACTIVITY

Carefully study Fig. 6.8 and describe the body language of the individuals at the meetings.

GOOD PRACTICE ▷

In order to maximise the business potential the manager must ensure that every practitioner organises, plans and makes full use of their time.

Team roles

Employees undertake two roles within their employment:

- the functional role – the job role
- the team role – the way in which they behave and relate to other members of staff.

The team role is very important as it can create an atmosphere, either conducive or not conducive to the business environment. It describes how the individual behaves, reacts, contributes and interrelates with everyone in the business. It is far more likely that team roles are moulded by individuals' personalities and learned behaviour rather than by actual technical skills and possessed knowledge.

In order for a team to perform well it is important that there is a good mixture of the different types of roles to balance and enhance each individual's performance. Ideally the perfect team consists of each of the different team roles categorised below.

Categorisation of different team roles

Completer
The completer is conscientious and will search out any errors or omissions and will always meet the time deadline.

Co-ordinator
The co-ordinator tends to be mature, trusting and confident and tends to act as the spokesperson or chairperson. They will outline the goals and promote decision making amongst the team.

Evaluator
The evaluator tends to be discerning, strategic and level headed, looking at all angles and options before assessing situations, diagnosing problems and choosing the best option.

Implementor
The implementor tends to be well disciplined, reliable, efficient and conservative in their approach. They will turn the ideas into actual actions or solutions.

Investigator
The investigator tends to be fairly extrovert, very communicative and enthusiastic. They will explore all the possibilities and develop lots of contacts. They need the stimulus of others to help build and develop their ideas.

Plant
The plant tends to be fairly unorthodox, imaginative and creative when left alone and needs an appreciative and sympathetic manager.

Shaper
The shaper tends to be very outgoing, dynamic and is usually highly strung. They will challenge things and seek their way around obstacles.

Specialist
The specialist tends to be dedicated and fairly single minded and is able to contribute technical skills or knowledge to the team.

Team worker

The team worker tends to be perceptive and accommodating, able to listen and work on ideas. They are sociable and will try to avoid friction.

Fig. 6.9 *Team roles*

GOOD PRACTICE ▷

- *Ensure that all staff have a thorough induction and feel welcome, involved and are confident with the standard procedures of the business.*
- *Actively involve all staff members.*
- *Take time to speak to all staff.*
- *Treat all staff the same and don't be tempted to favour any individual.*
- *Make an effort with new staff to review their progress as team members.*
- *Analyse your own team and if ineffective rebuild the team by adopting a style of management that suits the characteristics of the team. Also encourage the members of the team to draw on each other's strengths.*

Practical and effective management techniques

It is important for a manager to know and understand the members of their team as much as possible in order to establish their strengths and what motivates each one of them. Established theories clearly highlight that there are many different motivators and all human beings should be seen as individuals who will be motivated by what they consider to be their reward, e.g money, challenge, recognition etc. The manager must also bear in mind the effects of group as well as individual motivation.

Having analysed each team member it is essential for the manager to nurture an environment that will enable their staff to develop and grow as individuals and as a team, achieving their personal goals as well as the company's by effective use of motivators and interpersonal skills.

The structure of the payment scheme within a company is extremely important as money has been proven to be a key motivator and therefore the manager must establish a suitable system to obtain maximum profit for the company and a motivating fair reward for the efforts of the employees, e.g. commission rates on treatments and retail (see Chapter 8).

GOOD PRACTICE ▷

To develop staff commitment ensure that:
- *all staff fully understand the aims and objectives of the company and the relevance of these to their job role*
- *all staff are fully aware of what their job actually involves*
- *staff are involved as much as possible in setting the standards of the salon and that they all have the opportunity to analyse, review and discuss these standards and their importance to the salon, the clients and themselves*
- *staff are rewarded in some way for good work or ideas, e.g. praise, recognition,etc.*
- *staff are confident in the management and feel happy to raise queries without fearing criticism*
- *staff feel worthwhile in that they are given respect for the skills that they contribute and are supported in developing new skills needed by the salon.*

Working environment

Creating and maintaining a happy working environment is essential for a successful business. Some of the key points that the manager should consider when developing and maintaining this environment are:

1 Human characteristics such as:
   - trust
   - friendship
   - frankness
   - fairness
   - respect
   - loyalty
   - warmth and understanding
   - support
   - empathy.
2 Information mechanisms such as:
   - clear organisation structure
   - reporting systems
   - job descriptions
   - communication systems
   - appraisal system.

3 Development opportunities such as:
- identifying the need for development of technical and inter-personal skills.

4 Team work such as:
- creating and developing good team morale to motivate individuals to work effectively as team members for the good of the business
- developing awareness of how the team (the business) can compete effectively with other salons.

GOOD PRACTICE ▷ *When taking over an existing business it is useful to carry out an anonymous written survey of the staff's perception of the business.*

Thank you for taking the time to complete this confidential questionnaire. Please use the key provided and tick the column which you personally feel reflects your views.	Key				
	Always true	T			
	Usually true	M			
	Occasionally true	O			
	Seldom true	S			
	Never true	N			

	T	M	O	S	N
The atmosphere at work is pleasant to work in	☐	☐	☐	☐	☐
The working relationship amongst the manager, supervisors and staff is good	☐	☐	☐	☐	☐
If staff make occasional errors they are not criticised	☐	☐	☐	☐	☐
If staff work hard they receive praise from the management	☐	☐	☐	☐	☐
There is a clear organisation structure outlining all staff's in-line managers	☐	☐	☐	☐	☐
Each member of staff understands their job role	☐	☐	☐	☐	☐
Each member of staff is given an appraisal	☐	☐	☐	☐	☐
All staff are treated fairly and equally	☐	☐	☐	☐	☐
The management encourage staff to show initiative	☐	☐	☐	☐	☐
The management encourage staff to make decisions	☐	☐	☐	☐	☐
If I could find another job paying a higher salary I would leave	☐	☐	☐	☐	☐

Fig. 6.10 *Example of a staff analysis questionnaire*

Having analysed the views of the staff on the business environment the manager is then able to actually consider what they need to do to address any areas of concern or how they can maintain a happy effective working environment.

A manager must always be aware that they are also an individual and therefore susceptible to human traits such as insecurity, lack of motivation , being insular etc. In order to maintain their role effectively they need to review and improve their interpersonal and management skills from time to time. Key points for a manager to remember are the importance to the business of:

1 Staff development, including their own. It is very easy in service industries such as hairdressing, health and beauty to become insular as many practitioners work on their own or in very small teams. It is essential to mix with other professionals to share knowledge and experience to help each other build upon existing strengths.

A manager or owner needs to maintain awareness of their position and how they interact with their staff. It is obviously essential to build a confident working relationship with staff without becoming too involved with them, especially as at some time they may have cause to reprimand one of them. Finding a happy medium is often the most difficult thing for a manager or owner of small business to do as the size of the business draws them into very close working contact with their staff where it is very easy to become too friendly which can lead to the loss of their recognition as the 'boss'.

2 Changing ideas and trends and the effect of these on present and future business opportunities for their salon, including the influence of these on local competition. The manager or owner must consider the need for current or future investment in decor, products, equipment, human resources, marketing etc.

ACTIVITY

1 Consider each of the following terms which are often used to describe managers and leaders and decide if you have what it takes to be a manager:

- Experience
- Dedication
- Enthusiasm
- Loyalty
- Honesty
- Organisational skills
- Initiative
- Maturity
- Self-awareness
- Self-motivation
- Adaptability
- Effectiveness
- Flexibility
- Assertiveness
- Ambition
- Excellent interpersonal skills
- Discretion.

2 Outline which of the above are your strengths and which are weakness and draw up a plan to develop weaknesses into strengths.

Future trends and ideas

The world is a very large and diverse place and over the years it has become easier and quicker to communicate and travel internationally which has therefore enabled concepts, knowledge and trends to spread rapidly.

However, it is extremely important for business people to remember that no matter how quickly the world can communicate and transport products or equipment, the variety of cultures that make up the world, or market as it may be referred to, will often dictate differing interests in various areas of the country or even the world.

It is always possible to find a need, and then promote it, selling it on a short-term basis, but in order to sustain clear growth a firm business foundation must be developed and maintained.

In order for the owner or manager to achieve a successful market they must first try to forecast future trends and to do this they need to consider a number of questions:

1   What factors influences these trends?

2   Why are these factors important?

3   Do they remain static?

The first factor that will have a direct influence on future industry trends is the standards within the industry, so it is essential that the owner understands the standards within their individual industry. They also need to consider how these standards or levels of knowledge, understanding and skill will affect the particular market they are interested in.

POINTS TO NOTE ▷   *Contact national training organisations, professional associations and examination or awarding bodies to gain information on standards.*

Throughout the world practitioners can select to join one or more professional associations, either national or international of their choice, which will depend upon the benefits that the individual associations can offer their members, e.g insurance cover, information on new products, discounts on products, helpline,free marketing, regional meetings etc.

Professional associations tend to lay down a code of ethics or standards which they feel are required of people working in their professional service industry. These codes will generally relate to the professional behaviour of members and are there as guidelines for members to assist them in establishing acceptable standards and most importantly to help protect the public from improper practices. These codes will generally encompass such things as:

● upholding the dignity of the profession through the way in which members conduct themselves and their businesses

● respecting other professionals – including those that practitioners work with and for

● respecting the link with the medical profession, which within the health and beauty sectors has developed greatly over the last decade.

Most professional associations will state within their rules that they will take serious recourse against a member who is proven to disregard their code of ethics, as it is obviously essential that all members uphold these ethics for the professional credibility of their association.

The understanding of the importance of these ethics is paramount to the future of the health, beauty and hairdressing industries as they set their practitioners apart as professionals.

Culture is also an important influence on changing trends as without demand there is no market. In certain areas culture influences the trends in treatments offered and requested by clients. Culture creates trends in treatments by dictating the needs of clients and also reflecting practitioners' beliefs.

Social and economic climates will also affect future treatment and product trends so the owner should certainly bear this in mind. The past decade has seen an explosion within the western world of women's rights and this has ensured that many women have acquired high-profile jobs which in turn has influenced the social behavioural patterns and economic spending power of women. A clear example of this has been in the increase in treatments to improve total appearance.

Fashion trends also affect the market needs, e.g. if glossy magazines and fashion houses use slim models you can be certain that slimming treatments whether manual or mechanical will be popular, as will the style of make-up, hair, clothes and fragrances that reflect the current image. It must be remembered that fashion trends do have a habit of repeating themselves! It is amazing how many journalists when researching follow the trends of the fashion houses and can be strongly influenced by a view or comment of a present 'guru'. It is part of human nature to 'Follow the leader' whoever that might be!

Science and technology will also affect market trends. Glancing back at old journals, trade magazines and companies' promotional literature it is clear how science and technological advances have altered the services offered to clients.

Man's continual search for the elixir of youth has undoubtedly influenced the health and beauty sectors as for time and eternity it has been man's destiny to research and find the secret formula that will give eternal youth and prevent aging. Everyone longs for it to be discovered and hopes to be the one that finds it!

These influences are undoubtedly important for the business owner to recognise, as in order to keep ahead of the market they must be aware of the implications of these on the future market. Treatments, products and equipment will always fluctuate to meet public demand which is influenced by public awareness through the media, which in turn is often brought about by manufacturer's technology, marketing and advertising as well as through the social and economic climate. It is therefore clear that these influences, except for man's search for the elixir of youth and some cultural influences, will not remain static.

POINT TO NOTE ▷

Two key issues from today's society throw light on to manufacturer's considerations for future product and treatment developments:

- *the back to nature philosophy — as the western world demands environmentally friendly products the emphasis for the use of natural ingredients in packaging as well as product content is high and appears certain to remain so for the coming decade.*
- *technological demand — public demand for ultra-modern equipment appears to ensure that equipment manufacturers will remain active for the coming years, providing they address the issue of flexibility of use, reflect industrial needs and provide excellent service and back up support.*

GOOD PRACTICE ▷

The owner or manager must keep abreast of the changing market demand in order to maintain a successful business.

ACTIVITY

Research the future trends within:
(a) hairdressing
(b) beauty therapy
(c) complementary therapies.

Manager's checklist for staff motivation

1 What are the aims, objectives and standards of the business?
2 Are all staff fully aware of their job description and what is expected of them?
3 Is there a clear staff reporting system?
4 Are all staff aware of the staff reporting system?
5 Is there a scheduled programme for staff meetings?
6 Are all staff actively encouraged to participate in these meetings?
7 Are their contributions rewarded?
8 Do I know the strengths of and motivating influences for all the staff?
9 Are the staff working as a team?
10 Are all staff treated fairly?
11 Is there a suitable motivating pay structure in place?
12 Is there a mechanism for feedback to staff?
13 Is there an appraisal system?
14 Is there opportunity for staff development?
15 Does the business plan allow for future development, e.g investment in and promotion of new trends?

Managing the behaviour of staff

Communication skills are the essence of a service industry as without communication how would the client make an appointment, be made to feel welcome or explain what service they want? The importance of this skill and the variety of methods that can be used have been explained earlier in this chapter but it is essential to remember that managing staff's behaviour is part of the manager's responsibility. Behaviour is expressed through some of the forms of communication such as verbal and body language (non-verbal).

Fig. 6.11 *Body language: (**a**) welcoming receptionist; (**b**) unwelcoming receptionist*

As has been previously stated a successful business will have a pleasant working environment in which clients feel relaxed and confident; the manager needs to maintain this and to ensure that the behaviour of the staff reflects this environment at all times. But what happens if a member of staff behaves badly? There have to be mechanisms in place to deal with this (see disciplinary procedures in Chapter 4) and the manager needs tact and diplomacy to deflect a potentially harmful influence on the ambience of the business. Analysis of behaviour amongst children has highlighted the need to reward good behaviour rather than chastise them for poor behaviour. This reverse psychology can be used on adults by reinforcing recognition when they behave in an appropriate or the desired manner. It is thought that there is a trigger that promotes or motivates poor behaviour rather than a trigger promoting good behaviour. Research in children has shown that some children were motivated to behave badly as it brought about recognition, all be it a telling off by the parent. To see changes in this poor behaviour for the better often took a great deal of patience and time.

GOOD PRACTICE ▷ *The manager has to respond to any behavioural problems immediately or else they can have a detrimental effect through affecting the ambience and staff morale of the business.*

Power and its influence

Power can have a beneficial or detrimental effect on a business depending upon its weighting within the organisation and how it is used by the individual. Power can be defined as a firm base on which an individual can act. Power can be viewed by individuals in a number of ways, e.g. financial power or wealth, the quantity of authority (e.g. being responsible for a large team rather than a small one), or the contacts or connections that a person may have with others who are considered by the individual to be influential people.

The position and influence of power is very important within a business, in particular a large company. A new manager within a company can often come across problems due to control and effects of existing power, and they may need to establish a staged plan of action to alter the power structure. This action plan must allow for reducing the potential conflict that change often brings.

Roles of the manager

The manager of an organisation can be viewed in different roles:

1	Relationship role	as the person who acts as a figurehead, leader and co ordinator
2	Information role	as the person who monitors and disseminates information through various mechanisms
3	Decision-making role	as the entrepreneur addressing the needs of a successful business, the handler and negotiator of day to day duties and problems and allocating and planning human and physical resources
* **4**	Training role in the business	as the person interviewing, inducting and training the individuals
** **5**	Working role	as an experienced practitioner within the business

*in large companies this role is often the responsibility of the personnel department
**in large companies this role is not always part of the manager's job

It should also be noted that many small health and beauty business owners make the error of spending too much time in the treatment room rather than managing the business. It is much easier within a hairdressing salon to manage from the shop floor as the stylist, juniors and modern apprentices work together whereas in health and beauty the practitioners work in segregated rooms due to the nature of the personalised treatments being given.

POINTS TO NOTE ▷

- *The manager will act as a figurehead for the business and must reflect this position within it as well as outside when representing the organisation such as at social events, exhibitions, prize givings etc.*
- *The manager will act as a leader within the business through a variety of means, which may be formal or informal, to maximise the team spirit and ultimate success of the business.*

GOOD PRACTICE ▷ *A good manager will:*

- *set and maintain the required standards of the business*
- *through communication and training allow the staff to develop at a pace acceptable to them and the business.*
- *learn to delegate whilst participating with and supporting staff in their duties*
- *set and display a high standard of interpersonal skills as an example to the staff*
- *be loyal, firm and fair.*

Managing stress

Stress is one of the highest contributors to absence of staff from work and therefore it is paramount that the manager is aware of what possibly causes stress, the symptoms of stress and how to manage it.

Examples of possible causes of stress at work

1 Changes at work
2 Job roles, responsibilities etc. that are not clearly defined
3 Conflict between staff, which will affect all staff
4 Pressure of work, e.g shortage of staff, long hours,busy time of year etc.
5 Lack of management support
6 Threatening style of management
7 Effects of a poor economy

Examples of possible external stress factors

1 Death of a spouse
2 Divorce
3 Marital separation
4 Death of a close relative
5 Personal injury or illness
6 Marriage
7 Being sacked
8 Retirement
9 Moving house
10 Pregnancy
11 Change in financial circumstances
12 Vacations
13 Christmas

POINTS TO NOTE ▷ *The manager needs to identify possible causes of stress in their staff to try and alleviate it. This will hopefully prevent it from affecting their job, e.g if a member of staff is moving house it would be unwise to increase their pressure of work or make changes to their job at that time.*

Fig. 6.12   *Stress!*

Physical symptoms of stress
Some of the physical symptoms of stress are:

- tension headaches
- indigestion
- muscle tension
- dry mouth and throat
- tiredness
- menstrual problems
- diarrhoea/frequent urination
- constipation
- clumsiness.

Emotional symptoms of stress
Some of the emotional symptoms of stress are:

- rapid mood swings
- lack of concentration
- indecision
- feeling tearful.

Behavioural symptoms of stress
Some of the behavioural symptoms of stress are:

- sleep problems
- overeating or loss of appetite
- withdrawal from friends and work colleagues
- increase in smoking/alcohol intake.

POINT TO NOTE ▷   *Healthy diet and exercise are important in combating stress, as is learning to relax.*

ACTIVITY

1   List three examples of:
    (a) physical symptoms of stress
    (b) emotional symptoms of stress
    (c) behavioural symptoms of stress.

2   Consider the three most stressful events in your life and identify
    the symptoms that you suffered and how you overcame them.

Fig. 6.13 *'Fight or flight'*

Physiological effects of stress

When the mind is threatened in any way the body will automatically
respond by what is commonly called the body's 'fight or flight'
mechanism, i.e if a person is in a threatening situation such as being
physically threatened or emotionally threatened that they will lose their
job, their body will under go a variety of physiological effects:

- rate of breathing increases
- heart rate increases
- blood pressure increases
- in case of injury the blood clotting mechanism of the body is activated
- the body's stored sugar and fats are released to provide the body with
  the fuel it may need for energy
- the supply of red blood cells which carry oxygen around the body
  increases
- the process of digestion ceases, diverting the blood supply to the
  brain and muscles
- the muscles of the bowel and bladder loosen
- in preparation for activity the muscles of the body tense.

POINTS TO NOTE ▷   *If a manager can help staff to keep their stress levels down, this will ultimately
ensure that the manager's own stress level will be low.*

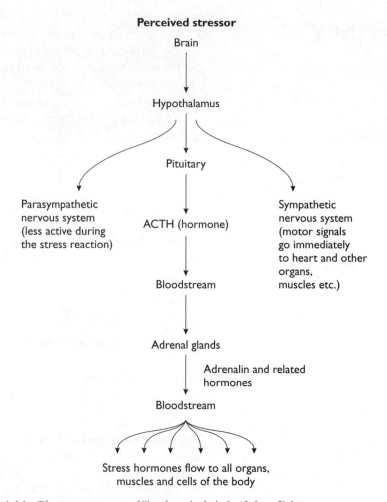

Perceived stressor

Brain

↓

Hypothalamus

Pituitary

Parasympathetic nervous system (less active during the stress reaction)

ACTH (hormone)

Sympathetic nervous system (motor signals go immediately to heart and other organs, muscles etc.)

↓

Bloodstream

↓

Adrenal glands

Adrenalin and related hormones

Bloodstream

Stress hormones flow to all organs, muscles and cells of the body

Fig. 6.14 *The stress responses mobilise the entire body for 'fight or flight'*

Total quality management (TQM)

Total quality management (TQM) is a modern title given to the techniques used within a business to continually monitor, evaluate and review the services offered. It provides quality provision for the consumer and ensures that the business operates smoothly and effectively.

GOOD PRACTICE ▷

Policy statements are used in many business to underpin a number of procedures. A quality control policy will influence systems such as monitoring, evaluating, reviewing and appraisal. A policy statement for equal opportunities will influence the recruitment of staff, training and administrative procedures. A policy statement on health and safety will influence fire drill procedures, accident procedures, the handling and storing of products and protective clothing.

ACTIVITY

Draw up a policy statement for:

1 Health and safety
2 Quality control

suitable for the following:

(a) a home visiting practice
(b) a small clinic.

POINT TO NOTE ▷

Management of time is often considered an important factor in handling stress, as in order to use time effectively the individual must be well focused and must prioritise efficiently.

Effective time management will help to streamline your work and make life more enjoyable.

GOOD PRACTICE ▷

● *In order to be an effective time manager it is important to understand your own work and rhythm patterns and remember that as you become a better planner the management of your time will develop more naturally.*

● *Sole traders must set regular time aside for tasks that have to be undertaken, e.g. book keeping – don't leave it until you receive a letter from the tax office as this will make life stressful and is very poor management!*

KEY TERMS

You need to know what these words and phrases mean. Go back through the chapter to find out.

Organisational theory
Motivation theory
Leadership theory
Communication mechanisms

Team roles
Stress management
Total quality management

7 Business terminology and financial management

This chapter covers the following areas:
➤ insurance
➤ taxation
➤ raising finance
➤ basic business terminology
➤ book-keeping and computerised account systems.

A certain amount of understanding of the terminology used in business is essential for the practitioner setting out on the self-employed route, together with an overview of how to manage finances. This chapter serves to illustrate the basic terms used and gives an insight into financial management in terms of basic book-keeping.

Insurance

Insurance is a way of protecting people and property against unforeseen circumstances. It is possible to insure against almost any risk for a sum of money called a premium. In return for this payment, should the risk which you are insuring against occur you will receive compensation to indemnify you for the loss (i.e. to put you back in the position you were in before the loss).

When operating in a business certain forms of insurance are compulsory by law, namely public liability and employer's liability.

Public liability

Public liability insurance covers claims relating to injury, disease or damage to the property of a third party (i.e. the client). It can be extended to cover liability arising out of goods sold or supplied or if the business involves work away from the premises.

Many professional beauty therapy organisations can arrange group cover. This is normally included in some form of membership fee which will generally encompass other benefits. This can be a much cheaper option than taking out insurance independently. It is sensible to look at having at least a one million pound cover against any injury arising out of the treatments offered and this is sometimes known as treatment risk.

Personal Claims in the UK is Big Business!

It is essential that Therapists and Salon Owners take every possible preventative measure to ensure that they do not add to the increasing statistics! Generally operators keep records for most of the treatments performed in the salon, however they often tend to omit waxing clients - leaving themselves extremely vulnerable.

Fig. 7.1   *Plan ahead*

POINTS TO NOTE ▷

- *Professional associations offer insurance cover to their members. This generally includes the standard group insurance with optional extensions for specific high-risk treatments. This generally works out much cheaper for the small business.*

- *It is essential that the insured reads their policy thoroughly and adheres to the set procedures, e.g. patch testing prior to tinting, to ensure the validity of the policy.*

Employer's liability

Any business employing staff is legally obliged to have employer's liability insurance. If an employee is injured at work it is normally the employer who is held responsible, whether personally at fault or not. The insurance certificate must be prominently displayed. Any injuries that do occur must be recorded in an accident book.

Other types of insurance

Although not compulsory by law, it is sensible to also have insurance to cover the following.

Theft

In case the premises are broken into, it is wise to have cover against theft of or damage to any equipment and products and against damage to the building itself through forced entry.

Ear Piercing Registration Book

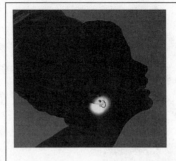

Fashionable range of 9ct & 18ct Gold and 24ct Gold Plated Ear Piercing Earrings

DATE:_____ NO: 128002

CUSTOMER NAME:_____

ADDRESS:_____

_____

_____

I confirm that to the best of my knowledge I do not suffer from the following medical conditions:- Diabetes, H.I.V., Circulatory Problems, Epilepsy or Hepititas, or that I am not taking any anti-coagulation medication.

I also confirm receipt of and understand the after care instructions.

I am over 18 years of age
If under 18, state date of birth: ___/___/___

SIGNED:_____
Parent or Guardian to sign if under 18

BRANCH USE

Piercing Performed By:_____
Style Used:_____
Sterility Tape Details:_____

DATE:_____ NO: 128002

Piercing Performed At:_____

_____

_____

_____

Customer's Name:_____

Piercing Performed By:_____

Style of Earring Used:_____

IMPORTANT

Please read and follow the After Care Instructions printed overleaf.

AFTER CARE PROCEDURE:-

A. Earrings should fit loosely. TIGHT EARRINGS PROMOTE INFECTION. If the earrings feel snug, loosen them, by grasping the front of the earring and then gently pulling the clutch toward the tip of the post until a slight click is felt.

B. Turn earrings completely around twice a day. DO NOT REMOVE THE EARRINGS.

C. Cleanse Earlobes twice a day. Use a clean cotton wool ball with Inverness Ear Care Solution.

D. Be sure all soap is completely rinsed from the earlobes after shampooing hair. Cover earlobes when using hair spray, spray cologne or hair colouring.

E. Leave the piercing earrings in for 6 weeks. For the first six months, do not go longer than 24 hours without earrings, otherwise the holes could begin to close.

F. Take extra care when removing clothing over the ears or when brushing hair so that earrings don't get caught. Exercise care when participating in sports.

Fig. 7.2   *Examples of ear piercing registration and home-care advice*

Damage to premises/stock and equipment by fire, flood etc.
Unforeseen circumstances such as fire or flooding could seriously affect a business not just for a few days but for weeks and this form of cover will compensate for the damage.

Loss of profits through damage to premises
This is extra cover to allow for compensation if the business cannot operate for a period of time due to extreme damage as in the case of fire, flooding etc.

Fidelity bonding
This is insurance cover to protect against the dishonesty of employees.

Personal accident and ill health insurance
Critical illness cover will insure you against the potential risk that you may at some time be unable to earn any income through ill health.

Personal accident cover works in exactly the same way. These policies are normally renewable annually.

Life assurance
This is an insurance policy that will pay out an agreed sum of money (normally index linked, which means that the amount rises with inflation) in the event of your death. Life assurance can sometimes be compulsory to secure a loan and in any case is certainly advisable if you have any dependants.

Taxation

Tax can be defined as a compulsory financial contribution imposed by the government in order to raise revenue to support the public services that are used and shared by everyone. There are many forms of taxation, e.g. on individual earnings, on the profits of a business, value added tax (VAT) and national insurance contributions, which are explained below.

The Inland Revenue

The Inland Revenue is the name given to the government department that administers and collects major taxes such as income tax. If you are self-employed they will need to know the nature of the business your are running and the name of your accountant. At the end of each trading year your business accounts will need to be forwarded to a tax inspector. Tax will then be calculated on the income less allowable business expenses. It is important to keep records for yourself and for your accountant and they must be true and accurate. If you employ people in the business you may have to deduct income tax and national insurance contributions from their earnings, together with paying the employer's share of the national insurance contributions.

Interest on business loans	Advertising costs
Insurance for the business	Rent
Depreciation of capital items such as cars, computers, equipment etc.	Heating and lighting
	Wages
Costs of any products that are used up in the course of business	Any specialist or protective clothing
	Subscriptions to professional associations
Hire of equipment for use in the business	

Fig. 7.3   *Examples of allowable business expenses*

Self-assessment

Self-assessment was introduced by the government in 1996 and it applies to all tax payers who are eligible to submit a tax return including the self-employed, employees who pay tax at the higher rate, company directors and anyone else with complicated tax affairs. The Inland Revenue has the ultimate power to examine discrepancies and can randomly sample tax returns for more detailed investigation.

Any person eligible for self-assessment is required by law to keep records of their income. These will normally need to be kept for at least 22 months after the end of the year to which they relate. You will be required to complete a tax form and either calculate the tax due yourself or send it in to the tax office for an inspector to calculate. If you wish the tax office to calculate any tax due you must submit your tax form by the 30 September each tax year or if you wish to do this yourself then you must submit it by 31 January. Any late returns will be penalised.

POINTS TO NOTE ▷ *The Inland Revenue have set up a national helpline for anyone with problems relating to self-assessment. The telephone number is 0345 161514.*
An employer's helpline has been jointly set up by the Inland Revenue and the Contributions Agency. The telephone number is 0345 143143.
The Inland Revenue have also set up a helpline for the completion of forms. The telephone number is 0645 000444.

National Insurance contributions

National insurance contributions (NICs) are paid by every working person to the Inland Revenue to support public services, the unemployed and to help towards the payment of a pension in old age. They should be collected by the employer in the case of employees. There are four classes of national insurance contributions.

Class 1

These are contributions for employed persons over the age of 16 and under 60 for women and 65 for men. They are earnings related and will be deducted from the salary by the employer along with income tax on the PAYE basis. The employee will be able to claim for sickness, invalidity, maternity , unemployment and widow's benefit where appropriate once sufficient contributions have been made.

Class 2

These are contributions to be paid by the self-employed. They can be paid either by direct debit through a bank or by quarterly bill. If earnings fall below the 'lower earnings limit' it may be possible to apply for exemption but entitlement to some of the benefits provided may be lost.

Class 3

These are voluntary contributions, which may be paid to retain entitlement to benefits in the future.

Class 4

These are additional contributions that may be made by the self-employed person and are calculated on the profits of the business. They may be required at the end of a tax year and are based on a percentage of the taxable profit of the business.

(More information on NICs is available from your local Inland Revenue office.)

Value added tax (VAT)

Value added tax (VAT) is a tax that is levied by the government on most business transactions known as 'taxable supplies'. If a business has a taxable turnover greater than £48 000 (current level) it must register for VAT by filling out the appropriate form from the VAT office. A registration number will then be issued and detailed records will need to be kept of all business transactions. The salon owner will need to charge VAT, currently standing at 17.5 %, on services provided and products sold, and will be liable to pay VAT on equipment and products purchased from VAT registered companies. These are referred to as outputs and inputs, respectively. Every three months (VAT tax period) it will be necessary to fill in a form known as a VAT return. Where output tax exceeds input tax the difference will need to be paid to customs and excise; where input tax is greater than the output tax then the difference may be reclaimed from customs and excise.

POINT TO NOTE ▷   *The government has the right to decide which products/services are liable to VAT charges. Those which are not liable are referred to as 'zero rated', e.g. books, newspapers, drugs, children's clothing and footwear etc.*

Raising finance

Raising finance is one of the first things that will need to be carried out when setting up a business. Many businesses fail to thrive through a lack of sufficient funding. The type of funding required will depend on the size of the venture but the main sources of funding are:

- a loan or loan capital, which is a 'lump sum' given to set up a business
- shares or share capital, which is finance raised from the selling of shares in a limited company
- current liabilities, which could be creditors.

Banking and finance in general is a highly competitive market but all finance companies are in business to lend money, so when you are thinking of starting up a business for yourself, unless you have independent financial backing, you will need to look at how the banks and finance companies can help. Banks offer one of the safest ways of raising capital but they will only lend money if they can be certain of getting it back. Before you approach the bank manager you will have to make sure you have done your 'homework' and be able to convince them that your business will work. They will want to know what makes you different from everyone else, why will people come to your salon, what qualities do you possess, what are you putting into the business as some form of guarantee and what are your contingency plans. They will expect to see a detailed plan of your business proposal including financial projections. Only once you have convinced them that you have the necessary drive and determination to succeed will they agree to a loan.

Business funding

It may be possible, depending on your circumstances, to get some form of funding from one of the various business set up funds that exist. These include the following:

The Prince's Trust

This initiative was set up by His Royal Highness The Prince of Wales and regularly gives loans and grants to young people who wish to set up a business venture. It especially looks to help people who live in more deprived parts of the country or who have been unemployed for a period of time.

The government

The government do provide a certain amount of help to businesses through the Department of Trade and Industry (DTI) and the Department of Employment, often working in conjunction with Training and Enterprise Councils (TECS). An example of government help is the Enterprise Allowance scheme.

The European Social Fund

This and other European sources can offer assistance to businesses and will look at all bids made.

The Scottish Enterprise Development Agency

This agency offers long-term loans to small businesses at very reasonable rates.

The Local Enterprise Development Units (LEDU)

LEDU offers funding to small businesses in the form of an initial lump sum to offset start-up costs followed by small monthly payments for up to a year.

Basic business terminology

Insolvency

This is a term used to describe either a business or a person who is unable to pay their debts (bankrupt).

Liquidation

This refers to the winding up of a business to pay of its debts. This is achieved by the sale of its assets.

Bank services and documents

Some of the services and documents offered by banks are outlined below.

Bank statement

A bank statement is a document issued by a bank to each account holder, normally on a monthly basis, showing all the transactions that have occurred for that period. It will detail how much money is in the account, how much has been put in and taken out. Most banks now offer computerised systems where you can request a statement yourself at a cash point by inserting your account card and personal identification number (PIN) at any time of the day.

Cheque guarantee card

The cheque guarantee card will be requested every time you write a cheque as it is a guarantee to the retailer that the bank will honour the cheque to the value shown on the card. If the card limit is for £50.00 then the bank will only honour a cheque drawn to that amount or less. Most cheque guarantee cards also offer 'Switch' facilities, which instantly debit your account via a computer system without the need to write out time-consuming cheques.

Credit card

Acredit card provides a method of paying for goods and services without cash. It can be used as a form of credit (in which case interest will be charged) or the amount can be paid off monthly.

A statement of account will be sent out detailing exactly how much you have spent each month.

Current account

This is a bank account that traditionally does not pay interest on any money deposited within it but does give the account holder a cheque book and cheque guarantee card to draw off the account. Some banks have now started to offer interest on current accounts as banking becomes ever more competitive.

Deposit account

This is a bank account that pays interest on any moneys deposited in it. There may be clauses attached as to how much notice needs to be given for withdrawals without forfeiting interest.

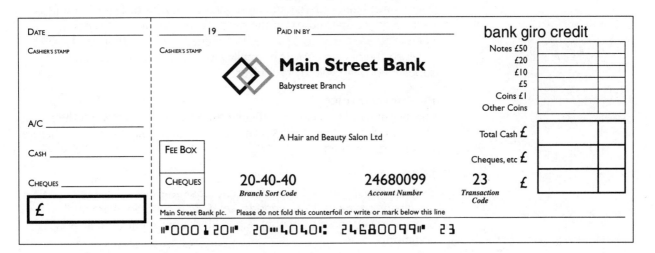

Fig. 7.4 A paying-in slip

Overdraft

The account holder and the bank agree a limit to which the account may be overdrawn giving a flexible form of finance. Interest will be paid on the amount borrowed.

Loan

This is a formal arrangement with a bank or financial institution allowing an agreed sum of money to be lent to the account holder for an agreed period of time. This is normally for a longer period than an overdraft.

Standing order

This is a method of paying for regular expenditures such as a bills. The bank will ask you to fill in a form detailing the person to whom payment is to be made, their bank details and the amount payable. This amount will then be deducted on a regular basis until the bank is notified otherwise.

Direct debit

This is similar to a standing order, but this time it is the person requesting the money who instructs the bank to deduct it from your account. You will need to fill out a mandate sanctioning the request. Direct debit is very useful where the sum involved may change from month to month.

Order documents

Advice note

This is a document sent by the supplier to advise the date when goods will be delivered.

Credit note

This is given by a supplier in exchange for faulty goods and is normally offset against the next invoice.

Delivery note

This document (which is often produced in triplicate) is issued when goods have been ordered and are packed ready for delivery. It itemises every product that makes up the order. When the driver delivers the goods you are asked to sign the document to confirm that you have received them. One copy is normally given to you, one retained by the supplier and one held by the driver.

Pro-forma invoice

This document is issued in particular for a new customer when their credit worthiness is not yet known. It requests payment for goods before they are dispatched.

Invoice

This is a document that is sent once goods have been delivered requesting payment for the goods. Terms and conditions are applied in relation to settling the account, e.g. a 30 day payment term is fairly common.

Book-keeping and computerised account systems

When setting up in business it will be necessary to keep records of every transaction in a detailed and formal way. The reasons for this are firstly to have documentation of the business's financial position and secondly to allow for an interpretation of the results. It is important to be able to ascertain why things may not be going too well and to respond to them.

Whilst it is possible to buy 'off the shelf' book-keeping systems, many people who are not expert in the field contract the work out to specialists.

If you are going to undertake the role of book-keeper yourself then certain business documents and information will need to be entered into what are known as ledgers.

There are three ledger accounts:

- **sales ledger:** this gives the accounts of debtors (credit customers)
- **purchase ledger:** this gives the accounts of creditors (credit suppliers)

Wholesale Suppliers and Consultants to the Beauty and Hairdressing Professions

ELLISONS
Leading the way

INVOICE/DELIVERY NOTE

CRONDAL ROAD,
EXHALL,
COVENTRY. CV7 9NH
TEL: 01203 361619/362518
FAX: 01203 644010

VAT No: 487 6585 77

PRO-FORMA INVOICE

DELIVERY TO:
The Beauty Spot
18 Greensleeves Close
Whitmore Park
Coventry

CV6 4EP

INVOICE TO:
The Beauty Spot
18 Greensleeves Close
Whitmore Park
Coventry

CV6 4EP

INVOICE No.	ACCOUNT REFERENCE	ORDER No.			DATE
MP155428	THE4571	TJB	Page 1		13/01/97

CODE No.	DESCRIPTION	QTY	PRICE	DISCOUNT	VAT	TOTAL
EST990	Esthetix Electrolift Facial Therapy	1	795.00		S	795.00
EST990	Promotional Pack for EST990	1			S	
EST910	Esthetix 3 Tier Trolley Standard	1	125.00		S	125.00
EST918	Esthetix Multi Posture Stool	1	85.00		S	85.00
PHD01S	PhD Intro Kit With Small Gloves	1	160.00		S	160.00
DS977	Embossed Cotton Discs (500)	1	3.25		S	3.25
PE524	Galvanic Gel 5 Normal/Dry Skin	1	12.25		S	12.25
AM011	Pint Measuring Jug	1	0.80		S	0.80
AM008	Plastic Circular Bowl 6"	1	0.70		S	0.70
BO924	Mask Brush	1	1.95		S	1.95
GL035	Precious Touch Eye Gel 15ml	1	4.05		S	4.05

ELLISONS Leading the way

GOODS	CODE	RATE	VAT
1188.00	S	17.50	197.51

Settlement Discount 59.40

GOODS	1188.00
CARRIAGE	0.00
VAT	197.51
TOTAL	1385.51

PLEASE CHECK YOUR ORDER CAREFULLY,
CLAIMS MUST BE NOTIFIED WITHIN 3 DAYS.

Goods remain the property of E.A. Ellison & Co Ltd until full payment is received.

CUSTOMER ADDRESS
The Beauty Spot
18 Greensleeves Close
Whitmore Park
Coventry

CV6 4EP

REMITTANCE ADVICE
CHEQUE ENCLOSED ☐
PLEASE CHARGE TO MY
CREDIT CARD/ACCESS/VISA No:
EXPIRY DATE   SIGNATURE

INV. No.	ACCOUNT REF.	DATE
	THE4571	13/01/97

AMOUNT DUE	1385.51
IF PAID WITHIN 7 DAYS DISCOUNTED AMOUNT DUE	1326.11

LATE PAYMENT WILL NOT QUALIFY FOR DISCOUNT PLEASE SEND YOUR CHEQUE BY RETURN

Fig. 7.5 *Example of a pro-forma invoice*

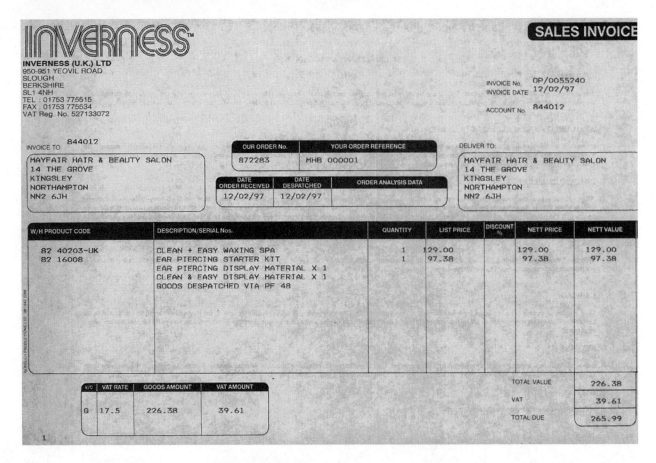

Fig. 7.6 *Example of an invoice*

- **general ledger:** this gives the accounts for sales, purchases, returns, income and expense accounts and asset and liability accounts. The cashbook, which consists of cash and bank accounts, is sometimes referred to in a separate section.

Drawing up the sales ledger

All businesses will be required to keep an account for each customer, or debtor as they are called. In the hair and beauty industry money is normally paid up front at the end of a treatment so the business should not have a situation where many customers owe money.

Drawing up the purchase ledger

The manager will need to be aware of what the business owes to suppliers. Although monthly statements may be received it is important to keep the business's own record up to date. The entries would be the opposite way round to those in the sales ledger.

Drawing up the general ledger

The manager will need to know the business's total sales, purchases and returns for any one year of trading. This information can be obtained from invoices and credit notes. First, the details from the invoices, credit notes, cheques, petty cash vouchers, paying-in slips, receipts, wage slips etc. will need to be entered into a day book. Each month the total from the day book should be entered or posted into the relevant accounts in the general ledger.

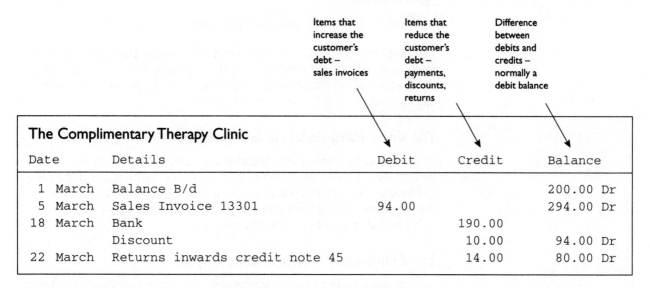

The Complimentary Therapy Clinic				
Date	Details	Debit	Credit	Balance
1 March	Balance B/d			200.00 Dr
5 March	Sales Invoice 13301	94.00		294.00 Dr
18 March	Bank		190.00	
	Discount		10.00	94.00 Dr
22 March	Returns inwards credit note 45		14.00	80.00 Dr

Fig. 7.7 (a) *Sales ledger account (debtors)*

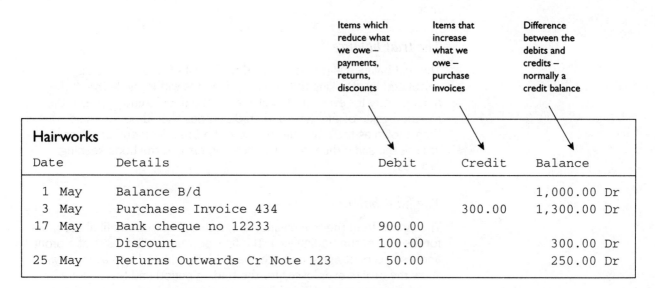

Hairworks				
Date	Details	Debit	Credit	Balance
1 May	Balance B/d			1,000.00 Dr
3 May	Purchases Invoice 434		300.00	1,300.00 Dr
17 May	Bank cheque no 12233	900.00		
	Discount	100.00		300.00 Dr
25 May	Returns Outwards Cr Note 123	50.00		250.00 Dr

Fig. 7.7 (b) *Purchase ledger account (creditors)*

The cashbook account

A cashbook account is two-sided with the left-hand column recording receipts (debit) and the right-hand column recording payments (credit).

Certain points need to be considered when filling out the cashbook:

- the date that the transaction took place
- where the money came from or where the money went to (if possible name the account). Cheque numbers, accounts references etc. should also be noted.
- was the money paid out of the business or received into it?

The cashbook will need to be balanced on a regular basis, e.g. monthly, and this means that the balances of the creditors and debtors accounts are worked out. The cashbook should show the difference between the amount paid in and the amount withdrawn.

The single-entry system of book-keeping

The single-entry system uses the standard practice of one entry column and, providing there are analysis columns in the cashbook and the petty cashbook, it is easy to total the income and expenditure to see where the money is coming from and going to. A profit and loss account can easily be calculated from this information.

The double-entry system of book-keeping

Double-entry systems take place between the ledger accounts and must clearly show that wherever there is a debit in one account there must be a corresponding credit in another account. The double-entry system expresses both sides of every transaction and two entries are made each time.

The trial balance

The trial balance is the name given to the list of balances that is calculated by checking the debits and credits within the ledger. If there is a debit entry for every credit entry, as in the double-entry system, then the total value of the debit and credit entries should be the same. This is then known as the trial balance and if the total debit and credit entries are not the same then there has been an error in the book-keeping process.

The final balance

The figures from the trial balance are used to draw up the final accounts for the end of the trading year. The final accounts will consist of a profit and loss account and a balance sheet. The profit and loss account will show the profits over losses for the trading period and this is done by calculating the total value of sales minus the total value of expenses incurred. The balance sheet will show the value of the business at the end of the trading period and this is calculated from its assets, liabilities and capital held.

The final accounts ultimately provide information about the financial performance of the business and will be of use for securing or maintaining finance in the future, for those people with a vested interest in the business and for monitoring business performance.

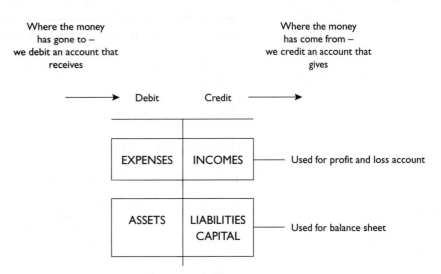

Fig. 7.8 (a) How the trial balance is structured

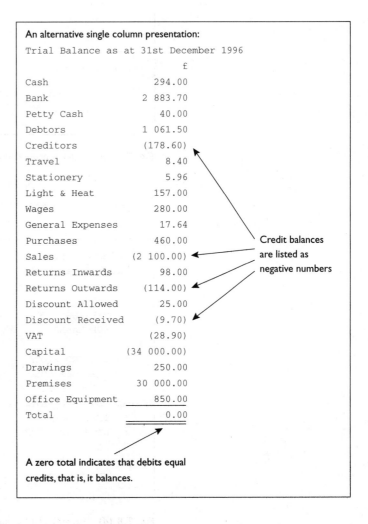

Balance as at 31st December 1996		
	£	£
Cash	294.00	
Bank	2 883.70	
Petty Cash	40.00	
Debtors	1 061.50	
Creditors		178.60
Travel	8.40	
Stationery	5.96	
Light & Heat	157.00	
Wages	280.00	
General Expenses	17.64	
Purchases	460.00	
Sales		2 100.00
Returns Inwards	98.00	
Returns Outwards		114.00
Discount Allowed	25.00	
Discount Received		9.70
VAT		28.90
Capital		34 000.00
Drawings	250.00	
Premises	30 000.00	
Office Equipment	850.00	
Total	36 431.20	36 431.20

An alternative single column presentation:
Trial Balance as at 31st December 1996

	£
Cash	294.00
Bank	2 883.70
Petty Cash	40.00
Debtors	1 061.50
Creditors	(178.60)
Travel	8.40
Stationery	5.96
Light & Heat	157.00
Wages	280.00
General Expenses	17.64
Purchases	460.00
Sales	(2 100.00)
Returns Inwards	98.00
Returns Outwards	(114.00)
Discount Allowed	25.00
Discount Received	(9.70)
VAT	(28.90)
Capital	(34 000.00)
Drawings	250.00
Premises	30 000.00
Office Equipment	850.00
Total	0.00

Credit balances are listed as negative numbers

A zero total indicates that debits equal credits, that is, it balances.

Fig. 7.8 (b) Example of a trial balance

```
Balance sheet of Beauty Rooms for year ending 31 March 1997

Fixed assets                      £           £
Shop fittings                               6,500
Motor vechicle                              4,000
                                           10,500  ←— Total fixed assets


Current assets
Stock                          1,000
Debtors                          200
Bank                           2,700
Cash                             400
                               4,300
Less current liabilities
Creditors                      1,000
Working capital                             3,300  ←— Current assets – current liabilities
Total assets                               13,800
Less long term liabilities
Bank loan                                   5,000
Net assets                                  8,800  ←— Assets – liabilities owner's worth


Financed by
Capital (at start)                          8,000  ←— Capital as it was at start
Add net profit                              1,000  ←— Net profit – owner's reward
                                            9,000
Less drawings                                 200  ←— Money drawn by owner
                                            8,800  ←— What the owner is worth now
```

Fig. 7.8 (c)   *Example of a balance sheet*

```
Trading and Profit and Loss Account of Beauty Rooms for year
ending 31 March 1997
                                  £           £
        SALES                              10,000
        OPENING STOCK          2,000                    The calculation
        PURCHASES              5,000                    for the cost of
                               7,000                    goods sold is
less    CLOSING STOCK          1,000                    to the left
COST OF GOODS SOLD                          6,000
        GROSS PROFIT                        4,000
less    RENT AND RATES         1,500                    The individual
        INSURANCE                200                    expenses are
        LIGHT AND HEAT           800                    listed to the
        WAGES                    500                    left
                                            3,000
        NET PROFIT                          1,000
```

Fig. 7.8 (d)   *Example of a tracing and profit and loss account*

Computerised account systems

In today's world of developing technology the use of computers in business is becoming essential. Manufacturers of software programmes for computerised accounts have developed an array of programmes to suit a variety of organisations of different sizes and budgets. Two of the most popular market leaders are currently Sage and Pegasus, who offer account systems to suit everything from the small one-man-band business to the large multi-national company, enabling the account keeper to input and analyse statistical information as required.

Book-keeping terminology

Balance sheet

The balance sheet is a statement detailing all the assets and liabilities of a business.

Cash book

The cash book is used to record all payments and receipts on a daily basis together with what has been paid into and taken out of the bank account. It should be periodically checked against bank statements.

Petty cash

This is the term given to the small float of cash kept by most business to pay for small purchases immediately, e.g. for a taxi fare. Petty cash is often stored in a lockable cash box which is held by a person in authority. All transactions will need to be recorded in the petty cash book.

Petty cash book

This is a book for recording all minor cash transactions including the date, the amount of cash used and the purpose of the transaction.

Cash flow

Cash flow can be defined as the flow of money in and out of a business. A cash flow statement is compulsory for all companies. A business needs to have sufficient cash to enable it to carry out its day-to-day activities such as paying wages and buying stock. (This is sometimes called working capital.)

Cash flow forecast

This is the term given to an estimate of the cash position of a business over a forthcoming period, normally a trading year. It will be drawn up by calculating expected monthly income and expenditure. A cash flow forecast will be important if a company is looking to expand and needs to raise extra finance.

Venture capital

This is the term given to capital that may be invested into a company by either a wealthy individual or a venture capital trust (VCT), which is a PLC wishing to rechannel shareholder's money by reinvesting in a small company seeking finance. The small company will not be taking on new owners, it will merely be borrowing venture capital.

Gross profit

This is the term used to describe all the profit made before necessary deductions (e.g. tax) have been taken off.

Net profit

This is a term used to describe the final profit made after all necessary deductions (e.g. tax) have been made.

PAYE

Pay as you earn (PAYE) tax is applicable to all employees who earn over a specific limit as decided by the government. Earnings-related tax and national insurance contributions are deducted under the PAYE scheme by the employer.

BACS

This stands for Banks Automated Clearance System and is a scheme adopted by many companies as the method by which salaries are paid into an employee's bank account. It is an electronic transfer system.

Profit and loss account

This document summarises all business transactions for a given period (normally one year). It records the net business profits, which are the final profits made after costs have been taken into account. A profit and loss account will consist of sales minus the cost of goods sold, to give a gross profit, minus expenses to give the final net profit (see Fig. 7.8).

Depreciation

This is the term applied to a tax-allowable item, e.g. equipment, computer, car, which decreases in value year by year. Each year the claimant is allowed to deduct a percentage of the total cost to allow for depreciation.

Purchase day book

This allows you to keep a record of any moneys that you owe concerning purchases. It should also detail when goods were supplied and the date by which they must be paid for.

Wages book

This contains a record of the wage/salary details of every employee and will often include personnel information such as NI number, PAYE number, pension and other deductions.

ACTIVITY

Gather together information on book-keeping systems that can be purchased 'off the shelf' and compare these with the latest computerised account systems.

KEY TERMS

You need to know what these words and phrases mean. Go back through the chapter to find out.

Insurance	Business funding	
Taxation	Basic business terminology	
The Inland Revenue	Book-keeping	
Raising finance		

8 Management of the business

This chapter covers the following areas:
➤ analysing your position
➤ type of business
➤ buying an existing business
➤ formulating the business plan
➤ budgeting/achieving profit
➤ salary structures
➤ business analysis – the strategic plan
➤ pitfalls of business
➤ reviewing, evaluating and moving forward
➤ case studies.

Analysing your position

Once you have read through the chapters in this book, and decided on the type of business you wish to operate and the area in which you wish to be, you will need to carry out market research and thoroughly look at products, equipment ranges and the type of treatments to be offered. But have you really got what it takes to run your own business?

There are lots of reasons why people wish to become self-employed but many foolishly believe that they will be answerable only to themselves. This is a mistaken idea because your customers will effectively become your boss, together with a bank manager if you are going to have some kind of loan. You will need to be physically fit and should expect at least initially to work long hours. Any holiday taken will be without pay whilst the overheads remain.

You will need to have a strong personality if you are to weather some of the inevitable problems that will arise both in the setting up and the day-to-day running of the business. It will be necessary to remain highly motivated and well organised both for the paperwork that goes into running a business and the practical applications as well.

If you feel that you have got what it takes to run your own business you will need to be able to answer the following questions decisively:
● First, what form of business organisation will it be, i.e. are you going to start in a small way and become a sole trader or do you intend to open up a small salon/clinic?
● Why will people want to come to my salon/clinic?
● What type of people are going to be my customers?

155

- What type of treatments are likely to be popular?
- How many other business are offering the same services in the area?
- Do they offer anything more than I can?
- Could the area already be too saturated with this form of business?
- Is the intended situation of my business in a prominent enough place?
- What are the parking arrangements like?
- Is there sufficient public transport?
- Is it near to other shops and offices that may bring in extra business?
- Will people feel safe coming to the business in the evening when it is dark?
- How will I cope if the appointment book is quiet?
- What contingency plans can I put into action if I am taken ill?
- What would happen to me and to my personal assets if my business venture failed?

Type of business

When setting out on the business road most people have a clear idea of how they see themselves in a self-employed way. We can all envisage the inviting clinic and the colour scheme it will have, but logistics put a halt to most of these plans. Many people have to start in a small way and this can mean converting a room at home or developing a home-visiting (or mobile) service. Some scoff at the term mobile and it is true that there are difficulties to be found working in somebody else's home with possible distractions and journey times between homes. However, it is a relatively safe option in business terms in the sense that the start-up costs are quite small with the exception of the vehicle which most people have in any case. Home visiting will enable the practitioner to build up a client base which will eventually enable permanent premises to be sought. Many of the bigger clinics today started in such a fashion and certainly any prospective money lender would take things seriously if you already had a large client base. If you intend to work from home, then it is important to do things properly and this includes contacting your local authority as you may need to register your premises. It is also advisable to contact your insurance company as household contents insurance will need to be altered and the mortgage lender should also be informed where necessary.

Buying an existing business

There are lots of advantages to buying an existing business and probably the main one is that it should start to make money from day one because there is an established clientele. This is called the 'goodwill of the business' and can make things much easier initially. Also hopefully any early mistakes have been ironed out. One disadvantage may be that if the salon has suffered from any adverse publicity in the past, it could be difficult to iron out even under new management. Also clients can be quite fickle and just because they went to the salon under the previous owner does not automatically mean that they will come to you. If you intend to purchase an existing business you will need to check things very carefully and bear in mind the following points:

- Obtain access to the accounts of the business. You will need to see the profit and loss accounts for the most recent trading period

Fig. 8.1 *A home visiting practitioner*

together with documentation on the ordering of stock, which is always a good indicator of how well the business is doing.

- You will need to ascertain the reasons that the owner is selling.
- If any staff are employed in the business it is a very good idea to speak to them as legally you are obliged to keep existing staff on. This can also ensure continuity in the running of the salon/clinic.
- If possible try and speak to clients and find out what they think of the quality of care and standard of service offered.
- If the property is leasehold then you will need access to the lease agreement. Make sure that all the terms and conditions are favourable and in particular check whether any premium will be payable for a change of leaseholder.
- If you intend to buy the premises you will need to ensure that all the necessary legal formalities are observed.
- You will need to ascertain the age and condition of any equipment and stock valuation.
- Finally, you will need to satisfy to yourself as to the reputation and market potential of the business and how it could be improved if necessary.

If you feel confident about proceeding after checking out all the items above then the next step is to formulate the business plan.

Formulating the business plan

A business plan is a document detailing what the business is and how you see it progressing in both the long and short term. It should include the following information:

- what type of business it is going to be, e.g. a hairdressing salon, chiropractic clinic etc.

- the form the business organisation is going to take, e.g. sole trader, partnership etc.
- what costs are going to be involved in setting up. You will need to provide detailed information and not just approximations here
- what are the aims and objectives of the business, in particular for the future
- how do you see the business developing and how could it expand?
- how do you plan to operate the business in terms of location, treatment range, product ranges, costing of services etc.?
- how will you market the business and what is your budget for promotions, advertising and distribution etc.
- you will need to show detailed market research into setting up the business. This should take the form of data concerning the type of customers you wish to attract, the expected income from them and the expenditure on the services you will be offering and in the area in which you will operate.
- what you will need to achieve your aims, such as finance, employing people, insurance cover, purchasing and selling etc.
- forecasting will need to be shown, i.e. what are your projections and forecasts for the future on possible profit and losses, cash flow forecasts and balance sheets.

All this information will need to be compiled into a report which will enable you to view the potential business and put into perspective ideas for future developments and improvements by showing any areas of weakness. Many banks provide detailed documentation to help you compile a business plan.

Budgeting/achieving profit

Some form of budget plan will need to be formulated to demonstrate the amount of money required to run the business and where it will come from. Most businesses set a budget plan for a period of twelve months but technically it can be for any set period even for a short time such as a month. Most plans are kept fairly flexible to allow for changes in the business market, which could include seasonal changes, e.g. certain treatments being more popular at certain times of the year. A budget plan is essential if the business is to make some form of profit as ultimately it will give a clear picture of forecasted income and expenditure. It will ensure that capital is used wisely and as such a bank manager would expect to see the plan at periodic reviews. Finally, it will provide any employees with an insight into the costs of running the business and so help to promote economy and thrift in the use of materials etc.; this is something that is often overlooked.

The budget plan

The budget plan forecast needs to be set for a given period of time, e.g. one year, and then, using figures available from the previous year's trading (or in the case of a new business, projected income and expenditure figures), both production and sales budgets need to be planned.

BUSINESS DETAILS
Name of business
Address of business

Status of business
Type of business
Telephone
Date business began (if you have already started trading)
Business activities

PERSONAL DETAILS
Name
Address

Telephone (home)   Telephone (work)
Qualifications

                                                     Date of birth
Relevant work experience

Business experience

Details of personnel (if any)
Name   Name
Position   Position
Address   Address

Date of birth   Date of birth
Qualifications   Qualifications

Relevant work experience   Relevant work experience

Present income   Present income
What skills will you need to buy in during the first two years?

PERSONNEL
Estimate the cost of employing any people or buying any services you may need in the first two years?
Number of people   Job function   Monthly cost   Annual cost

(Remember to include you own salary and those of any you may have in this calculation.)

continued

Fig. 8.2 *An example of a business plan*

PRODUCT SERVICE

Description of type of products/services to be offered.

Contribution of individual products or services to total turnover

Product   Percentage contribution

                                                                     (The figures in this column should add up to 100.)

Break down the cost of materials (if any)
PRODUCT 1
Materials (including packaging, labelling etc.)   Cost

*Selling price for Product 1
PRODUCT 2

*Selling price for Product 2
PRODUCT 3

*Selling price for Product 3
(*These are assumptions)
Where did you get your estimate from?
Material   Source

MARKET

Describe your market

Where is you market?

Who are your customers?

Is you market growing, static or in decline?

Itemise the competitive products or services
Name of competitor 1
Competitor's product/service
Name   Price
Strengths   Weakness

Name of competitor 2
Competitor's product/service
Name   Price
Strengths   Weakness

Name of competitor 3
Competitor's product/service
Name   Price
Strengths   Weakness

continued

Fig. 8.2   *An example of a business plan (continued)*

What is special about your product or service?

Advantages of your product or service over competitor 1

Competitor 2

Competitor 3

What is your sales forecast for the
*1st three months?   Total value
Treatments/products
*2nd three months?   Total value
Treatments/products
*3rd three months?   Total value
Treatments/products
*4th three months   Total value
Treatments/products
(*These are assumptions)

Explain how you have calculated these estimates

Give details of any firm orders you have already taken

MARKETING
What sort of marketing do your competitors do?
Competitor 1

Competitor 2

Competitor 3

What sort of marketing or advertising do you intend to do?
Method   Cost

Why do you, think that these methods are appropriate for your particular market?

Where did you get your estimates from?
Method   Source

PREMISES/EQUIPMENT/PRODUCT
PREMISES:
Where do you intend to locate the business and why?

What sort and size of premises will you need?

What are the details of any lease, licence, rent, rates and when is the next rent review due?

continued

Fig. 8.2 *An example of a business plan (continued)*

What equipment and products do you require?

Is equipment bought or leased and how long is the life span?

On what terms will the products be purchased?

RECORDS
Describe records to be kept and how they are to be kept up to date?

OBJECTIVES
What are your personal objectives in running the business?
Short-term

Medium-term

Long-term

How do you intend to achieve them?

What objectives do you have for the business itself?
Short-term

Medium-term

Long-term

How do you intend to achieve them?

FINANCE
Give details of your known orders and sales (if any)

	Date	Orders/sales	Details	Delivery date
I				
2				
3				
4				

Give details of your current business assets (if any)

	Item	Value	Life expectancy

continued

Fig. 8.2 *An example of a business plan (continued)*

What will you need to buy to start up and then throughout your first year?

Start up

Item   Value

Year 1

Item   Value

How will you pay for these?   Value   Date

Grants

Own resources

Loans

Creditors

What credit is available from your suppliers?

Supplier   Estimated value of monthly order   Number of days credit

What are your loan or overdraft requirements?

What are you putting in yourself?

What security will you be able to put up?

OTHER

Accountant
Address

Telephone

Solicitor
Address

Telephone

VAT registration
Insurance arrangements

Fig. 8.2   *An example of a business plan (continued)*

The production budget

This is really the expenditure of the business and will detail the materials required to run the business together with equipment needed and 'man hours' involved.

The sales budget

This is the income of the business and to a certain extent can only be a forecast. It will aim to show estimates for the amount of treatments and retail products sold in any given period, which is normally broken down month by month.

Using these budgets

If the calculations are correct then the sales budget should always be greater than the production budget otherwise the business will be running at a loss and urgent action is called for.

Salary structures

One of the greatest expenses for most businesses is the wages bill because naturally staff have to be paid for any work done. It is good practice in any business to place jobs into market groups which are affected by the same external pressures. This means that a receptionist without practical treatment skills would have his/her pay calculated differently to that of a highly skilled practitioner. One of the main problems is calculating what is the market wage rate for a specific job. This can sometimes be found by checking the local press for similar jobs advertised, although salaries are not always stated. In the beauty and holistic therapy industries specifically there are no wage guidelines published. The government however sets minimum wage levels to prevent exploitation. It is important to remember that if you want good staff and wish to keep them they will expect favourable rates of pay and conditions.

Incentives

A business can only afford good rates of pay if it is making a healthy profit. One of the ways in which you can encourage staff to work harder and generate profit is to offer 'performance related pay' whereby bonus payments are made over and above a base salary if more work has been achieved or targets have been met. Some companies offer commission on sales whereby any retail product sold earns the employee a percentage of the amount sold. This is also sometimes given on treatments. Whatever the incentive offered, it is essential to ensure that the business can truly afford it and that the business generated more than covers the costs involved.

Business analysis – the strategic plan

All business need to have some form of strategic plan if they are to remain successful. The main objective of writing such a plan is to implement the same awareness and commitment from the top person downwards. The strategic plan is best kept simple, providing a clear framework for more detailed business analysis. It should include the following key elements.

The mission statement

This is the long-term aim of the business, how it sees itself and what it intends to become. It should be relevant to everyone concerned with the business and should differentiate the business from its competitors.

Goals or aims

These should be a more detailed breakdown of the key points of the mission statementand may include such things as:

- what makes the business unique and sets it apart from its competitors?
- what is its market and product package?
- how does the company see itself in relation to the market share?
- what is its expected profit margin?
- what are the shared values and beliefs of the company?

Performance measures

Goals set should be achievable and so milestones known as 'performance measures' need to be recorded and reviewed at specific points.

Functional strategies

The term 'functional strategies' describes the practical ways in which the goals will be achieved. They should encompass every member of the team.

The strategic plan will only work if everyone is committed towards making it work and this will only happen if communication channels are open and positive feedback is given where due. It needs to be regularly reviewed.

Pitfalls of business

It may seem strange to include a section on pitfalls of business in a book that is intended for those who wish to set up a business or who have a business already. However, it is important to acknowledge that many businesses fail within the first year of trading and often the reasons for failure could be rectified if action was taken earlier. There are many reasons for a business venture not working out and the following gives an overview of the more common problems.

Lack of finance

Many businesses fail because people are too cautious and do not borrow enough money initially. The bank manager may be quite happy to lend money but will be less impressed if you return in three months time with cash flow problems. Therefore it is important to plan your cashflow forecasts in a realistic way.

Poor management skills

You may be an expert therapist or hairdresser but if you cannot manage the business and its finances properly then problems could arise. It is worth investing in some training and development or employing specialists in weak areas if you can afford to do so.

Incorrect marketing

If marketing and promotion do not reach the correct targets then the business may suffer, so it is important to carry out proper market research for your intended business at the setting up stage.

Lack of advertising

It is necessary to invest a certain amount of money in advertising to make people aware of your services and what you have to offer. Word of mouth will not be enough initially.

Inadequate staff recruitment and training

A business is only as good as the people who work in it and so well qualified and enthusiastic staff will go a long way to ensuring the success of the business. Look after staff, listen to their needs, regularly update their skills and offer incentives to ensure a harmonious working environment.

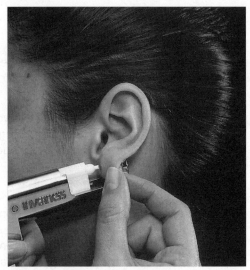

Fig. 8.3 *Ear piercing training*

Location of the business

It goes without saying that the more prominent the position of the business the more likely people are to know you exist. In an ideal scenario a shop window would greatly help in the promotion of goods and services to intice clients through the door. However, if you are upstairs then an eye-catching sign would be a good investment.

Remaining static

The business that allows itself to evolve and meets the changes in market pressure is more likely to succeed and continue to succeed than the one which remains static. It is important to follow strategic plans and to regularly update the business plan.

Reviewing, evaluating and moving forward

Once you have decided that you are going ahead and have formulated the business plan the next step is to arrange interviews with various financial institutions to raise finance. Most banks and building societies have advisors who are specialised in the setting up of a small business and will be able to tell you clearly if you have a viable proposition. They will also be able to provide you with all the information you require. It is important that you 'sell yourself' at any meeting with a bank manager in much the same way as you would at a job interview. You have to demonstrate that you are competent, hard-working and able to run your own business and that you will be able to take the inevitable knocks along the way. After all the bank manager has to weigh up how safe a risk you are to lend money to, with the main priority being to get the money back at the end of the day.

However, if you do feel that you have the right attributes to run you own business then there is nothing more rewarding than putting your plans into action and finally achieving your aim. It is a real accomplishment to see all that hard work finally pay off and to have a business that is generating a healthy profit and maybe employing people. GOOD LUCK!

Case studies

The following case study activities have been set for you to complete, whether you are already in business or are thinking of setting up on your own. In all cases you should apply them to the context in which you operate whether this is as a hairdresser, beauty therapist or complementary practitioner.

CASE STUDY 1 ▷

The mission statement
This is an example of a mission statement for a holistic therapy clinic called 'Natural Health'. Study this example and then write a mission statement for your clinic or salon.

'Natural Health is a clinic offering a range of complementary therapies for adults of all ages and backgrounds. It exists to promote well being and to deal with a whole host of stress-related symptoms. The clinic is open from 9 a.m. to 9 p.m. six days a week and aims to meet the needs of the working individual as well as those with a more flexible time structure. Appointments can be made by directly phoning the clinic and we also accept referrals through local doctors within the borough.'

CASE STUDY 2 ▷

Aims and objectives
When setting up a business it is essential to have clear aims and objectives in relation to how you see the business developing. Write down the aims and objectives that you think are important in setting up your own business.

CASE STUDY 3 ▷

Financial and time constraints
Time and finances pose the biggest problems in the setting up of a clinic or salon. List all the ways in which you think it is possible to raise finance for such a venture. Write down your ideas on how time can be managed most effectively.

CASE STUDY 4 ▷

Choice and type of premises
List the ten most important points to be considered in choice and type of premises for your business. Design a plan of what you consider to be

167

the perfect layout for your particular business. Then when you finally go out to view potential premises see if at least eight out of the ten criteria are met.

CASE STUDY **5** ▷

Services to be offered

Gather together as many brochures as possible from salons and clinics offering the kind of treatments you intend to offer. Decide what constitutes a good pricelist and what does not. Using ideas from these examples, design your own leaflet and ask family and friends to give feedback.

CASE STUDY **6** ▷

Products and equipment

Visit as many product suppliers as possible and compare and contrast the goods and service offered.

CASE STUDY **7** ▷

Health and safety

Write out a health and safety policy to be adopted by your clinic or salon. It should ensure that all reasonably practical steps are taken to protect everyone who uses the clinic.

CASE STUDY **8** ▷

Recruitment

Design an advertisement for a junior therapist to be employed on a full-time basis in your clinic. Quote the basic requirements of the job and the qualities required. Take into consideration equal opportunities.

Design an advertisement for an apprentice hairdresser following the same style.

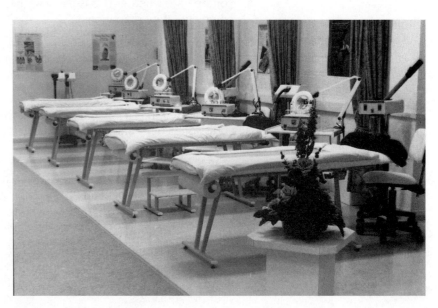

Fig. 8.4 *College training centre*

CASE STUDY **9** ▷

Appraisal

In your opinion what are the main benefits of appraisal and how should it be best carried out? Draft an appraisal form to be adopted by your company, or if you are to be the appraise, draft a suitable checklist to take into the appraisal interview with you.

CASE STUDY **10** ▷

Corporate image
Look at the corporate images of some of the most successful businesses and see why you think they are so successful.

Fig. 8.5 *Training school*

CASE STUDY **11** ▷

Marketing strategies
Give the most important ways of marketing a business of a practical nature. What marketing strategies are likely to work for your business?

CASE STUDY **12** ▷

Advertising
The example below represents a bad advertisement. What is wrong with it and how could it be improved?

'Come to Hair by Edith for a new look. Guaranteed client satisfaction. We offer the best treatments in town. Tel. 0161 233 4567 for an appointment.'

CASE STUDY **13** ▷

Management style
List ten important qualities that you would expect in a good manager. Now draft a job description for a salon manager fitting the criteria you have just listed.

CASE STUDY **14** ▷

Communication
Why is communication so important in the running of a business? How could it be improved in your salon or clinic?

Fig. 8.6 *Training seminar room*

CASE STUDY **15** ▷

Insurance
Check that you have adequate insurance cover in all aspects of your business and check that every member of staff is properly insured for all the treatments that they offer.

CASE STUDY **16** ▷

Management of the business
If you are intending to set up your own business, write a list of all your strengths and weaknesses. How could you overcome any of the weaknesses that you have listed?

CASE STUDY **17** ▷

Formulating a business plan
Most banks offer business starter packs which include business plan documentation. Gather a few from your local banks, choose the one which suits you best and set to work on writing a plan.

CASE STUDY **18**: ▷

Strategic planning
Write a strategic plan for your business or intended business.

CASE STUDY **19** ▷

Naming the business
Think about an appropriate name for your business. Check that no one else is using it and that it gives a clear message of what and who you are.

CASE STUDY **20** ▷

Checklist
Make a checklist of all the items necessary in order to set up in business. This should include everything from the choice and type of premises to the actual formulation of the business plan. If you are put off at this stage by the work involved, then you need to consider carefully whether being self-employed will be right for you.

Fig. 8.7 *A beauty salon*

KEY TERMS

You need to know what these words and phrases mean. Go back through the chapter to find out.

Business plan
Budgeting/achieving profit
Budget plan
Production budget
Sales budget

Salary structures
Incentives
Business analysis
Pitfalls of business

Glossary of terms

Advertising, promotion and publicity – Forms of presenting goods and services to potential markets in order to encourage sales.

Altering premises – Changing the use or layout of premises.

Animal parasite – A tiny creature living on or within another from which it derives nourishment.

Appraisal – Review of an employee's performance over a given period.

Autoclave – A pressure cooker type vessel that is used as a means or sterilisation for metal implements in particular. It works on the principle of high steam pressure.

Bacteria – Single-celled vegetable organisms capable of causing disease (pathogenic).

Basic business legislation – The legal requirements which need to be observed when setting out in business.

Basic business terminology – The main jargon used in business.

Book-keeping – The records kept of all transactions made within the business.

BIA – The Beauty Industry Authority.

Budget plan – A forecast of production and sales budgets.

Budgeting/achieving profit – Formulating a plan to ensure that overspending does not occur.

Business analysis – The aims and objectives of the business.

Business funding – Obtaining finance from specific bodies who will delegate funds to business ventures.

Business plan – A document detailing what the business is and how it should progress in both the long and short term.

Business name – The name given to identify a particular business.

Buying – The term used to describe the purchasing of something with the emphasis on ownership.

Choice of products/equipment – The range of products and equipment needed to offer the range of services.

Choice of services – The range of treatments to be offered in the salon/clinic.

Communication – To exchange or make known feelings by speech, writing , mannerisms or other means.

Communication mechanisms – The media available for communication.

Contract of employment – A written statement provided by the employer to the employee detailing terms and conditions of employment.

Co-operative – A business that is owned and controlled by the people working in it.

Corporate identity – The uniform image of a company or business.

COSHH – Control of substances hazardous to health regulations.

Costing of services – The process of working out how much to charge for services depending on overheads, labour costs and profit margins.

Disability discrimination legislation – A piece of legislation to protect against direct or indirect discrimination on the grounds of disability.

Disciplinary procedures – Procedures that exist for dealing with the misconduct of an employee.

Employer – The person with overall control of the well being and efficient running of the business.

Employment legislation – The necessary legalities that employers and employees need to observe.

Fire precautions – The awareness of fire and evacuation procedures.

Franchise – A business relationship whereby the operator of the business pays the owner of a business formula an agreed sum of money to operate in the same style.

HTB – The Hairdressing Training Board.

Incentives – Motivating factors for employees, normally in the form of increased pay in order to obtain greater productivity.

Induction – A formal introduction to familiarise a new employee with the operations of the business.

Inland Revenue – The government department that administers and collects taxes.

Insurance – A way of protecting people and property against unforeseen circumstances.

Interview selection – The process of short-listing potential candidates for interview.

IT – Information technology, i.e. the use of computers.

Key skills – Core skills required to work within the chosen professional environment.

Leadership theory – The principle of what constitutes a good leader.

Limited company (private and public) – A private limited company is formed with a minimum of two shareholders and requires lengthy legal formalities to create. A public limited company is a type of business arrangement that requires a minimum of seven shareholders with shares being floated on the stock market.

Listening skills – The art of allowing another person to 'offload' problems.

Manager – The person who leads the other employees on a day-to-day basis.

Marketing – The way in which a business is promoted in order to create demand.

Motivation theory – The principle of encouraging work.

NTO – National Training Organisation.

Numeracy/literacy skills – The skills of arithmetic and reading.

NVQs – National Vocational Qualifications.

Organisational structure – The way in which a business is run with regard to the roles and responsibilities of all personnel.

Organisational theory – The principle of management theory.

Partnership – Where two or more people go into business together, possibly with a partnership agreement, but without any lengthy legal formalities.

Personal and interpersonal skills – These are the life or key skills which are essential attributes when working in a service industry.

Personal presentation – The way in which one presents oneself with regard to dress, hygiene etc.

Pitfalls of business – Awareness of what can go wrong within a business and ways of avoiding these problems or dealing with them.

Production budget – The projected expenditure of the business.

Property advisors – Estate agents, surveyors and solicitors all involved in assisting in the buying and selling of property.

QCA – Qualifications and Curriculum Authority (from October 1997; formerly the National Council for Vocational Qualifications).

Quality and customer service – The value which the business gives to all aspects of dealing with customers.

Raising finance – The ways and means of collecting enough funds to open or sustain a business.

Receptionist – The first point of contact that a person has with a business.

Recruitment – To take on one or more employees.

Renting – Payments are made periodically by a tenant to a landlord for the occupation of premises or use of land etc.

Retailing – The sale of goods either individually or in small quantities.

Salary structure – The way in which the salaries for all employees are calculated.

Sales budget – The projected income of the business.

Salon layout – The organisation of the salon premises to ensure efficient working practices.

Sanitiser – A unit designed to kept sterilised items free from bacteria.

Sex discrimination legislation – A piece of legislation to protect against direct or indirect discrimination on the grounds of the sex of the individual.

'Six pack' – New health and safety at work legislation covering six points.

Social skills – The skills needed to mix with people such as communication, listening and personal presentation.

Sole trader – A person engaged in business on their own, with total control of all decisions and finance.

Staff development – The process of updating the skills of staff.

Sterilisation and disinfection – The process of destroying harmful bacteria and toxins.

Stress management – The way in which an individual deals with stresses and strains.

Stock and stock control – The total amount of goods/products kept on the premises and the monitoring of this.

Sub-leasing – This is the term used when an existing tenant leases the property or part of it to a third party.

SWOT analysis – The analysis of strengths, weaknesses, opportunities and threats to a business.

Taxation – A compulsory financial contribution imposed by the government.

Team roles – The way in which employees behave and interrelate.

Termination of employment – The severance of a period of service.

Time and motion – The length of time it takes to move from one area to another, which affects the efficient use of time.

Time management – The way in which an individual manages their time whilst at work.

Total quality management (TQM) – The techniques used within a business to continually monitor, evaluate and review the services offered in order to offer good quality.

Treatment and consumer legislation – Legislation related to products and services within the business and its environment.

Unfair dismissal – Unreasonable grounds for the termination of an employee's service.

Viruses – Microscopic organisms which can cause disease such as influenza, chickenpox etc.

Index

Accidents (within the workplace) 73
Advertising 97, 102–5
Advice note 146
Alderfer (ERG Theory) 116
Altering premises 7
Animal parasites 25
Antiseptic 29
Appointments
  reception 42–7
  recording appointments 45–7
  taking messages 44–5
  telephone enquiries 43–4
Appraisal 67–70
Aseptic 29
Autoclave 26–7
Autocrat 120

BACS 154
Bacteria 24, 26
Balance sheet 152
Bank statement 144
Basic legislation, see Business
    legislation
Body massage treatments (local
    bylaws) 87–8
Book keeping
  BACS 154
  balance sheet 153
  cash book 153
  cashbook account 149
  cash flow 153
  cash flow forecast 153
  computerised account systems
      153
  depreciation 154
  double entry system 150
  final balance 150
  general ledger 148
  gross profit 153
  net profit 154
  PAYE 154
  petty cash 153
  petty cash book 153
  profit and loss account 152, 154
  purchase day book 154
  purchase ledger 146, 148, 149
  sales ledger 146, 148, 149,
  single entry system 150

trial balance 150,151
venture capital 153
wages book 154
British Standards Institution 89–90
Budgeting
  achieving a profit 158
  budget plan 158
  incentives 164
  production budget 164
  sales budget 164
  salary structure 164
  strategic plan 164
Business
  analysing your position 155
  budget plan 158
  buying an existing business 156
  formulating the business plan
      157–63
  funding 143–4
  goals or aims 165
  mission statement 165
  needs of 31–2
  organisational structure 32
  performance measure 165
  pitfalls of 165–7
  reviewing and evaluating 167
  standards of 49
  type of 156
Business arrangements
  co-operative 5
  franchise 4–5
  limited company (private and
      public) 3–4
  partnership 2
  sole trader 1–2
Business legislation
  accidents within the workplace 73
  British Standards Institution
      89–90
  Data Protection Act (1984) 90
  Consumer Credit Act (1974) 89
  Consumer Protection Act (1987)
      89
  Consumer Safety Act (1978) 89
  Control of Substances Hazardous
      to Health Regulations
      (COSHH) (1988) 75–8
  Disability Discrimination Act (1995)

8, 82–3
disciplinary procedures 85–86
Electricity at Work Regulations Act
    (1990) 8, 73–74
Employment Rights Act (1996)
    83
Environmental Health and Trading
    Standards Departments
    (EHTS) 89
Environmental Protection Act
    (1990) 82
Equal Pay Act (1970) 82
EU directive on ingredient listing
    91
Fire Precautions Act (1971) 74
fire fighting equipment 74
Health and Safety at Work Act
    (HASAWA) (1974) 73
Health and Safety (First Aid)
    Regulations (1981) 80
health and safety legislation – 'the
    Six Pack' (1992)
  Display Screen Regulations
      79
  Management of Health and
      Safety at Work Regulations
      78
  Manual Handling Operations
      79
  Personal Protective Equipment
      at Work Regulations 79
  Provision and Use of Work
      Equipment Regulations 79
  Workplace Regulations 79
in-salon entertainment 90–91
Landlord & Tenant Act (1954) 8
Law of Property Act (1995) 8
local bylaws concerning body
    massage treatments 87–8
Local Government (Miscellaneous
    Provisions) Act (1982) 88
maternity rights 85
Misrepresentation Act (1967) 84
Office of Fair Trading (OFT) 88
Offices, Shops & Railways Act
    (1963) 8
Prices Act (1974) 89
Race Relations Act (1976) 82

Reporting of Injuries, Diseases and Dangerous Occurrences Regulations 1985   82
Resale Prices Act 1964, 1976   89
Safety Representative and Safety Committees Regulations 1977   80
Sale and Supply of Goods Act (1994)   88
Sex Discrimination Acts (1975, 1986)   82
Statutory Sick Pay   84
Trade Descriptions Act (1968, 1972)   89
termination of employment and redundancy   87
unfair dismissal – Employment Protection (Consolidation) Act 1978   87
Business name, choice of   7
Business plan   157–163
Business terminology
   advice note   146
   bank statement   144
   book keeping   146
   cheque guarantee card   144
   credit card   145
   credit note   146
   current account   145
   deposit account   145
   delivery note   146
   direct debit   146
   insolvency   144
   invoice   146, 148
   liquidation   144
   loan   145
   orders   146
   overdraft   145
   pro forma invoice   146, 147
   standing order   145
Buying   6
Buying an existing business   156

Calculative   113
Cashbook   153
Cashbook account   149
Cashflow   153
Cashflow forecast   153
Chemical methods of sterilisation   28
Cheque guarantee card   144
Choice and type of premises   5–7
Coercive   113
Communication   35
Communication mechanisms   121–2
Competitive trends   99
Completer (team role)   123

Computerised Account Systems   153
Computerised reception   23–4
Computerised systems   23
Consultative leaders   120
Consumer Credit Act (1974)   89
Consumer legislation, see treatment and consumer legislation
Consumer Protection Act (1987)   89
Consumer Safety Act (1978)   89
Contingency model   120
Contract of employment   61–6
Co-operative   5
Coordinator (team role)   123
Core skills   35–41
Corporate image   92
Corrosive   75
COSHH (Control of Substances Hazardous to Health) Regulations 1988   75–8
Costing of services   95–7
Credit card   145
Credit note   146
Culture   129
Current account   145

Damage to premises, stock and equipment   140
Data Protection Act (1984)   90
Delivery note   146
Democrat   120
Deposit account   145
Depreciation   154
Direct debit   146
Disability Discrimination Act (1995)   8, 82–3
Disciplinary procedures   85–6
Disease, protecting against   25
Disinfection   29
Display, see stock
DTI (Department of Trade and Industry)   144

Economic climate   99
'E' factors   112
Electricity at Work Regulations Act (1990)   8, 73–4
Elixir of youth   129
Employer, roles and responsibilities   33
Employers' liability   139
Employment
   appraisal   67–70
   contract of   61–6
   induction   63–7
   staff development   70
   written statement of   61–2

Employment legislation
   accidents within the workplace   73
   Control of Substances Hazardous to Health Regulations (COSHHH) (1988)   75–8
   Disability Discrimination Act (1995)   8,73–4
   disciplinary procedures   85–86
   Electricity at Work Regulations Act (1990)   8, 73–4
   Employment Rights Act (1996)   83
   Environmental Protection Act (1990)   82
   Equal Pay Act (1970)   82
   Fire Precautions Act (1971)   74
   fire fighting equipment   74
   Health and Safety at Work Act (HASAWA) (1974)   73
   Health and Safety (First Aid) Regulations (1981)   80
   health and safety legislation – 'the Six Pack' (1992)
      Display Screen Regulations   79
      Management of Health and Safety at Work Regulations   78
      Manual Handling Operations   79
      Personal Protective Equipment at Work Regulations   79
      Provision and Use of Work Equipment Regulations   79
      Workplace Regulations   79
   maternity rights   85
   Misrepresentation Act (1967)   84
   Race Relations Act (1976)   82
   Reporting of Injuries, Diseases and Dangerous Occurrences Regulations (1985)   82
   Safety Representative and Safety Committees Regulations (1977)   80
   Sex Discrimination Acts (1975,1986)   82
   Statutory Sick Pay   84
   termination of employment and redundancy   87
   unfair dismissal – Employment Protection (Consolidation) Act (1978)   87
Employment Protection (Consolidation Act) 1978   87
Employment Rights Act (1996)   83
Entertainment, in-salon   90–1
Environmental Health and Trading Standards (EHTS)   89

Environmental Protection Act (1990) 82

Equipment, guidelines for choice of 14–15

Equity shares 3

ERG Theory – Alderfer 116

ESF (European Social Fund) 144

EU directive on ingredient listing 91

Evaluator (team role) 123

Explosive 75–7

Fidelity bonding 140

Final balance 150

Finance
  business funding 143
  European Social Fund 144
  government 144
  local enterprise development units 144
  Prince's Trust 143–4
  raising 143
  Scottish Enterprise Development Agency 144

Fire fighting equipment 74

Fire Precautions Act (1971) 74

First aid 81

First aid box 80

Franchise 4–5

Fungi 25

Future trends and ideas 127–8

General ledger 148

Glass bead sterilisers 28

Goldthorpe's Affluent Worker Theory 117

Gross profit 153

Harmful 75–8

Hawthorne Studies 115

Health and Safety (First Aid) Regulations (1981) 80

Health and Safety at Work Act (HASAWA) (1974) 73

Health and Safety (Display Screen Equipment) Regulations 1992 79

Health and safety legislation – the 'Six Pack'
  Display Screen Regulations 79
  Management of Health and Safety at Work Regulations 78
  Manual Handling Operations 79
  Personal Protective Equipment at Work Regulations 79
  Provision and Use of Work Equipment Regulations 79
  Workplace Regulations 79

Herzberg's Two Factor Theory of Motivation 114

Highly flammable 75–6

Hygiene
  animal parasites 25
  bacteria 24, 26
  fungi 25
  protecting against disease 25
  sterilisation and disinfection 26–9
  viruses 24

Ill-health insurance 140

Implementor (team role) 123

Incentive (motivation) 114

Incentives 164

Induction 63–7

Information technology 40

Inland Revenue 141

In-salon entertainment 90–1

Insolvency 144

Insurance
  damage to premises, stock and equipment by fire, flood etc. 140
  employers liability 139
  fidelity bonding 140
  life assurance 141
  loss of profits through damage to premises 140
  personal accident and ill health 140
  professional associations 139
  public liability 138–9
  theft 139

Interpersonal skills 35–41

Interviews
  interview procedure 58–9
  interview questions 59–60
  recruiting 48–55
  selecting applicants 55
  shortlisting 55–7

Intrinsic 114

Investigator (team role) 123

Invoice 146

Irritant 75

Job advertisement 48

Job application form 52–3

Job description 54

Job enrichment 119

Key skills 35–41

Kite marks 89–90

Laissez-faire leader 120

Landlord and Tenant Act (1954) 8

Law of Property Act (1995) 8

Leader, qualities of 33–4

Leadership
  communication mechanisms 121–2
  team roles 123
  trait theories 120
  styles of 120

Legislation, see Business legislation

Life assurance 141

Life skills 35–41

Limited liability 4

Liquidation 144

Listening skills 36

Literacy 40

Loan 145

Local bylaws concerning body massage treatments 87–8

Local Enterprise Development Agency 144

Local Government (Miscellaneous Provisions) Act (1982) 88

Locus of control 115

Loss of profits through damage to premises 140

McClelland 116

McKinsey's Seven S's 118

Manager, roles and responsibilities 33–4, 132–3

Management
  checklist for staff motivation 130
  leadership theories 120–1
  managing staffs behaviour 131
  managing stress 133–6
  motivation theories 113–22, 125–30
  open book 119
  practical and effective techniques 124–9
  roles of the manager 132–3
  team roles 123–4
  total quality management (TQM) 136–7

Management of Health and Safety at Work Regulations (1992) 78

Manual Handling Operations Regulations (1992) 79

Marketing 94–109

Marketing mix 94–100

Marketing plan 100–101

Marketing strategies 101–108

Maslow's Hierarchy of Needs 112

Mass and micro marketing 101–102

Maternity rights 85

Miscellaneous Provisions Act (1982) 88

Misrepresentation Act (1967) 84

Mission statement 165

Motivation
  checklist for staff motivation 130
  NACH (Need to achieve)
    McClelland 116
  non-traditional theories 119–20
  theories 111–13
  traditional theories 114–18

National Insurance 142
National Training Organisation 128
Net profit 154
Non-traditional motivation theories
  job enrichment 119
  open book management 119
  quality circles 119
Non-verbal communication 35
Numeracy 40

Office of Fair Trading (OFT) 88
Offices, Shops and Railway Premises
  Act (1963) 8
Old stock 20
Open book management 119
Orders
  advice note 146
  credit note 146
  delivery note 146
  invoice 146
  pro forma invoice 146
Ordinary shares, see Equity shares
Organisational skills 40
Organisational structure 32
Organisational theory 110–111
Overdraft 145
Oxidising 75

Partnership 2
PAYE 154
People leader 120
Personal accident insurance 140
Personal presentation 36–8
Personal Protective Equipment at
  Work (PPE) Regulations
  (1992) 79
Personal skills 35–41
Petty cash 153
Petty cash book 153
Pitfalls of business 165–7
Plant (team role) 123
Political trends 99
Power and influence 132
Practitioner, roles and responsibilities
  of 41
Preference shares 3
Premises
  altering premises 7
  buying 6
  choice and type of 5–7

property advisors 6
renting 6
sub-leasing 7
Prices Act (1974) 89
Prince's Trust 143
Private limited company 3
Proactive 34
Products
  choice in beauty therapy 14–15
  choice in hairdressing 16
  choice in holistic therapies 16
Product knowledge 17
Production budget 164
Professional associations 128, 139
Profit, achieving a 158
Profit and loss account 152, 154
Pro forma invoice 146, 147
Promotion, forms of 97, 102–8
Property advisors 6
Provision and Use of Work Equipment
  Regulations (1992) 79
Public limited company (PLC) 3
Publicity 108
Public liability insurance 138–139
Purchase day book 154
Purchase ledger 146, 148, 149

Quality and customer service 94
Qualities
  of a beauty therapist 39
  to look for in employees 35–41
  of a hairstylist/junior/modern
    apprentice 39
  of a leader 33–4
Quality circles 119

Race Relations Act (1976) 82
Reactive 34
Receptionist, roles and responsibilities of 41–6
Recording appointments 45–7
Recruitment
  contract of employment 61–6
  interviews 58–61
  job advertisement 48
  job application form 52–3
  job descriptions 54
  redundancy 87
  routes 50
  setting the standards of the
    business 49
  short listing 55–7
  written statement of employment
    61–2
Renting 6
Reporting of Injuries, Diseases and
  Dangerous Occurrences
  Regulations (1985) 82

Resale Prices Act (1964,1976) 89
Retail area, sales 16–18
Retailing
  maintaining stock and the retail
    area 19–23
  products and services 16–17
Retail stock 13, 16–17
Roles and responsibilities of
  the employer 33
  the manager 33–4, 132–3
  the practitioner 41
  the receptionist 41–6
  support staff 47

Salary structure 164
Sale and Supply of Goods Act (1994)
  88
Sales
  budget 164
  maintaining stock and the retail
    area 19–23
  retailing products and services
    16–17
  retail stock 13, 17
  sales and sales pointers 17–18
  successful selling 17
Sales ledger 146, 148, 149
Salon layout
  for the beauty and holistic
    therapist 10–11
  for the hairdresser 11–13
Safety Representative and Safety
  Committees Regulations
  (1977) 80
Safety standards 89–90
Sanitisers 27
Science and technology 129
Scottish Enterprise Development
  Agency 144
Selecting applicants for interviews
  55
Selling, see Sales
Self assessment 141–2
Services, to be offered 13–14
Sex Discrimination Acts (1975 &
  1986) 82
Shaper (team role) 123
Shares, types of
  ordinary or equity shares 3
  preference shares 3
Shareholders 3–4
Short-listing job applicants 55–7
Social and economic climate 129
Social skills 38
Sole trader 1–2
Social trends 99
Specialist (team role) 123
Staff development 70

Staff recruitment   48–66
Standing order   145
Statutory Sick Pay (SSP)   84
Sterilisation and disinfection
   antiseptics   29
   autoclave   26–7
   chemical methods of sterilisation
      28
   disinfection   29
   glass bead sterilisers   28
   sanitisers   27
Stock
   display stock   19
   maintaining stock and the retail
      area   19–23
   old stock   20
   retail   13
   retailing products and services
      16–17
   sales and selling pointers   17–18
   stock control   20
   stock records   20
   successful selling   17
   unpacking stock   20
Stock control   20
Stock records   20
Strategic plan   164
Stress
   behavioural symptoms of stress
      134
   causes of stress at work   133
   emotional symptoms of stress
      134
   external stress factors   133
   managing stress   133–6
   physical symptoms of stress   134
   physiological effects of stress   135
Sub-leasing   7
Support staff   47
SWOT Analysis   98–100

Symbols used for substances
      hazardous to health   75
Taking messages   44–5
Taylor, principles of scientific
      management   114
Taxation
   Inland Revenue   141
   national insurance   142
   self assessment   141–2
   value added tax (VAT)   142–3
Team work   123
Team roles
   completer   123
   co-ordinator   123
   evaluator   123
   implementor   123
   investigator   123
   plant   123
   shaper   123
   specialist   123
   team worker   124
Team worker (team role)   124
Technological demand   130
Technological trends   99
Telephone enquiries   43–4
Termination of employment and
      redundancy   87
Theft   139
Time and motion   13
Time management   40
Toxic   75
Trade Descriptions Act (1968 & 1972)
      89
Trading standards   89–90
Trait theories   120
Treatment and consumer legislation
   British Standards Institution
      89–90
   Consumer Credit Act (1974)   89

Consumer Protection Act (1987)
      89
Consumer Safety Act (1978)
Data Protection Act (1984)   90
Environmental Health and Trading
      Standards Departments
      (EHTS)   89
in-salon entertainment   90–1
local bylaws concerning body
      massage treatments   87–8
Local Government (Miscellaneous
      Provisions) Act (1982)   88
Office of Fair Trading (OFT)   88
Prices Act (1974)   89
Resale Prices Act (1964, 1976)   89
Sale and Supply of Goods Act
      (1994)   88
Trade Descriptions Act (1968, 1972)
      89
Trial balance   150, 151
TQM (Total Quality Management)
      136–7

Unfair dismissal   87
Unpacking Stock   20

VAT (Value Added Tax)   142–3
Venture capital   153
Verbal communication   35
Viruses   24
Vroom's expectancy theory   117

Wages book   154
Working as a member of a team   36
Workplace (Health, Safety and
      Welfare) Regulations (1992)
      79
Written disciplinary procedure   85–6
Written statement of employment
      61–2